The Residue of Dreams

(cover) Illustration 1. *Orchid and Rock* (1992).

THE RESIDUE OF DREAMS

✻ ✻ ✻

Selected Poems of Jao Tsung-i

Translated by

Nicholas Morrow Williams

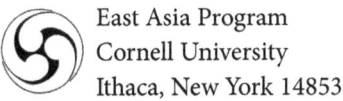

East Asia Program
Cornell University
Ithaca, New York 14853

The Cornell East Asia Series is published by the Cornell University East Asia Program (distinct from Cornell University Press). We publish books on a variety of scholarly topics relating to East Asia as a service to the academic community and the general public. Address submission inquiries to CEAS Editorial Board, East Asia Program, Cornell University, 140 Uris Hall, Ithaca, New York 14853-7601.

Number 182 in the Cornell East Asia Series
Copyright ©2016 Cornell University East Asia Program. All rights reserved.
ISSN 1050-2955
ISBN: 978-1-939161-62-8 hc
ISBN: 978-1-939161-82-6 pb
ISBN: 978-1-942242-82-6 ebook
Library of Congress Control Number: 2016931570

CAUTION: Except for brief quotations in a review, no part of this book may be reproduced or utilized in any form without permission in writing from the author. Please address inquiries to Nicholas Morrow Williams in care of the East Asia Program, Cornell University, 140 Uris Hall, Ithaca, NY 14853-7601.

In memoriam
MARGOT LOINES WILKIE (1912–2013)

First reader of these translations,
friend to poets, and follower of the Way

Contents

Prefatory Note	xv
List of Illustrations	xvii
Introduction	1
Biographical Sketch	2
Jao as Poet	5
Overview of Genres and Sources	9
Conventions of This Translation	13
I. TAKING REFUGE	**17**
To the Tune of "Gaoyang Terrace"	19
Various Poems on the Double-Ninth Day	20
Ballad of Yaoshan	22
Mankind Day	24
Sent to My Elder Yu Ruizheng	25
The Winter Solstice	27
Essay on Horse Manure	28
Essay on White Clouds	31
II. WESTERN PARALLELS	**35**
On the Ruins of the Colosseum in Rome	36
On First Entering the Mountains	38
Mont-Blanc	40
Mont-la-ville	42
Two Poems about Auvergne	43
Lac de Guery	*43*
Lac Pavin	*43*

Reading Nietzsche's *Also Sprach Zarathustra*   44
Reading the Poetry of Rimbaud   47
At the Tomb of Rainer Maria Rilke   49
Visiting Victor Hugo's Former Residence in the Jardin des Feuillantines   50
Recalling Lake Léman   52
Queens Town   53
On the Grand Canyon   54
Cheung Chau Collection #44   56

III. EASTERN VISIONS   57

On the Night-Blooming Kaḍupul   58
Recalling Xuanzang at Kanchipuram   59
On the Inscriptions by Scribes at the End of Each Scroll from Dunhuang   60
On Lake Toba   61
Taj Mahal   62
Visiting Angkor Wat at Night   63
To the Tune of "Courtyard Full of Fragrances": Recollections at Angkor Wat   65
To the Tune of "Path through Terraces and Cities": When I Imagine the Palaces of Immortals …   66
Written to Express My Sorrow at Seeing Men Beg for Food As in Ancient Times at the Mouth of the River Ganges   68
Sequel to the Ballad of the Beauty   69
To the Tune of "Hundred-Word Air"   70
To the Tune of "Charms of Niannu": On Mount Fuzhou   72
Inscribed on the Wall at Mogao Grotto   73
Dazaifu   74
Mourning the Dead at the Peace Park in Hiroshima   75

IV. STORMS   77

Cheung Chau Collection #16   78
Ancient-Style Verse in Pentasyllabic Meter for My Collection "Ice and Charcoal"   79
Sleepless Night after Night in Wind and Rain   80
To the Tune of "Sixth-String Air"   81

	To the Tune of "Gathering Mulberries": A Gardener in the Hills Gives Me a Narcissus Flower	82
	To the Tune of "Rake's Song": An Allegory	83
V.	**TWO RHYME-MATCHING SETS**	**85**
	Matching the Rhymes of Du Fu's "Autumn Meditations"	86
	Latter Ten Poems on Drinking Wine, Written to Match Fang Mizhi's Poems Matching the Rhymes of Lord Tao	95
VI.	**ALONE**	**107**
	Cheung Chau Collection #80	108
	To the Tune of "Frosty Leaves Fluttering": On Willows	109
	To the Tune of "Little Hills Doubled": On Plum Blossoms	111
	Seeing the Moon in the Hills	112
	To the Tune of "Wu men": Matching the Rhymes of Wang Yisun's "Sense of Snow"	113
	To the Tune of "Silk Fishing Line"	114
	Late Stirrings for Hsüan-t'ang	115
VII.	**ON PAINTING**	**117**
	To the Tune of "Sparse Shadows": On a Painting of Plums for Li Fengbo	119
	Quatrains Inscribed on Paintings	120
	More Quatrains Inscribed on Paintings	128
	Inscribed on My Own Landscape Paintings	132
	Inscribed on a Painting of Orchids by Ma Shouzhen: Variation on a Line of Rongfu's	133
	Essay on Cloudgazing	134
	To the Tune of "Recalling the Sound of Panpipes on the Phoenix Terrace": On the Withering of the Azalea	136
	To the Tune of "Spring Comes from Heaven Above": For Painting Master Tang Yun	137
	To the Tune of "Lips Dotted with Rouge": Inscribed on Tang Yun's Painting of Flight to Yaoshan	138
	To the Tune of "Bodhisattva Barbarian"	139

To the Tune of "Charms of Niannu": For a Collection of
My Calligraphy and Painting 140
To the Tune of "Music for Welcoming Spring": On a Polychrome Brick Mural
of Human Figures in the Collection of the Boston Museum of Fine Arts 142

VIII. THE SOUND OF THE QIN 143

To the Tune of "Eight Voices in Ganzhou" 145
To the Tune of "Evening Moon in Spring on the Xiang River" 146
To the Tune of "Severe Cold Syncopation" 147
To the Tune of "Prelude to a Water Melody" 149

IX. ON POETRY 151

Cheung Chau Collection #18 152
Cheung Chau Collection #62 153
Cheung Chau Collection #82 154
To the Tune of "Butterflies Admiring Blossoms": Playfully Composed on an
Offering of Paper Flowers 155
To the Tune of "Bodhisattva Barbarian": Crooked Cap Songs 156
To the Tune of "Whole River Red": On Reading the Poetry of Li He 157
The Poetic Mind 159
To the Tune of "Regret in the Damask Court" 161
To the Tune of "Passing the Towers of Qin" 163

X. ON SCHOLARSHIP 165

To the Tune of "Lips Dotted with Rouge": For My Chuci Bibliography 166
To the Tune of "Butterflies in Love with Flowers": For My Painting on the
Translation of *Dream of a Red Chamber* by David Hawkes 167
Essay on Crabs 168
Encomium for the Mawangdui Silk Manuscript of the
Book of Changes 171

XI. DREAMS — 175

- To the Tune of "Fragrant Grass Waves": Recording a Dream — 177
- To the Tune of "Washing Creek Sands" — 178
- To the Tune of "Bitter Longing" — 179
- To the Tune of "Jade Mansion Spring" — 180
- Playful Rhymes on Traveling to the Moon — 181
- Dreaming of Return — 182
- To the Tune of "The Beauty Yu": On Not Seeing the Moon at Mid-Autumn 1955 — 183
- Waking Up from Sleep — 184
- Dreaming of Heaven — 185
- To the Tune of "Fragrance of Angelica and Orchid Prelude": On Shadow — 187
- To the Tune of "Spring Resentment in the Boudoir" — 188
- To the Tune of "Flower-Strewn Path": On Red Tea — 190
- To the Tune of "Six Scoundrels": On Sleep — 192
- To the Tune of "Flower-Strewn Path": On the Self — 193
- To the Tune of "Jade Candles Renewed": On Spirit — 194

Bibliography — 197

- Selected Publications by Jao Tsung-i — 197
- Selected Studies of Jao's Life and Poetry — 197
- Other Works Cited in Notes — 198

Prefatory Note

I am grateful for the support of two recently founded institutions within Hong Kong Baptist University: the Jao Tsung-I Academy of Sinology and the Mr. Simon Suen and Mrs. Mary Suen Sino-Humanitas Institute. In particular, Chen Zhi, director of the Jao Tsung-I Academy of Sinology, encouraged me to begin this translation and supported it throughout. The translation was expedited by the help of my talented research assistant Zhang Yulong, whom I was able to hire through the support of a Faculty Research Grant from Hong Kong Baptist University. My colleague Timothy W.K. Chan generously read an early draft of the entire manuscript and commented in great detail. I am also grateful for the corrections provided by David and Taiping Knechtges, Wang Guojun, Martin Lai, Meng Fei, and Cheng Yuhei. Errors or misinterpretations that remain are entirely my own responsibility.

Citations to Jao's writings as *Wenji* are to page numbers in volume 20 (*juan* 14) of *Rao Zongyi ershi shiji xueshu wenji*, which contains Jao's classical prose and verse compositions. This collection supersedes earlier publications as the most convenient compilation for students of Jao's poetry.

All Chinese characters are romanized in the Pinyin system, with three exceptions. Jao achieved an international reputation in the 1960s, when the Wade-Giles system was still widely used, so his English name follows the Wade-Giles romanization: Jao Tsung-i instead of Pinyin Rao Zongyi. For consistency I also use Wade-Giles romanization for the name of Jao's father Jao O (Pinyin Rao E), as well as for Jao's pen name Hsüan-t'ang (Pinyin Xuantang).

Within the main text, Jao's original prefaces are printed in roman type, while the translator's comments and introductions are in italics.

List of Illustrations

All illustrations are paintings by Jao Tsung-i himself. I am grateful for permission from Professor Jao to reprint the images in this book.

Illustration 1: *Orchid and Rock* (1992)	cover, ii
Illustration 2. *Yaoshan Waterfall* (2004)	23
Illustration 3. *Lotus and Couplet* (2002)	39
Illustration 4. *Grand Canyon* (1980s)	55
Illustration 5. *Angkor Wat* (1982)	64
Illustration 6. From a Series of *Eight Immortals* (2000)	108
Illustration 7. *Plum Blossom in Double-Line Style* (1994)	118
Illustration 8. *Trees by the Stream* (1980s)	123
Illustration 9. *Playing the Qin* (1970s)	144
Illustration 10. *Crab and Wine* (1991)	170
Illustration 11. *Scenery of Southern China* (2004)	186
Illustration 12. *Bamboo and Rock* (1995)	196

The illustrations have also been published previously in the following collections:

1. *Xianggang daxue Rao Zongyi xueshuguan cangpin tulu I*, #35
2. *Rao Zongyi yishu chuangzuo huiji*, vol. 3, #65
3. *Rao Zongyi yishu chuangzuo huiji*, vol. 4, #12
4. *Rao Zongyi yishu chuangzuo huiji*, vol. 2, #46
5. *Rao Zongyi yishu chuangzuo huiji*, vol. 2, #24
6. *Rao Zongyi yishu chuangzuo huiji*, vol. 6, #89
7. *Rao Zongyi yishu chuangzuo huiji*, vol. 5, #68
8. *Rao Zongyi yishu chuangzuo huiji*, vol. 4, #97
9. *Rao Zongyi yishu chuangzuo huiji*, vol. 6, #36

10. *Rao Zongyi yishu chuangzuo huiji*, vol. 5, #62
11. *Rao Zongyi yishu chuangzuo huiji*, vol. 3, #63
12. *Xianggang daxue Rao Zongyi xueshuguan cangpin tulu I*, #40

Introduction

> Jao's poems comprise a modern melody summoning back from the past the soul of traditional China.
>
> —Hu Xiaoming[1]

Though Chinese poetry has undergone countless transformations since its origins in the *Book of Songs* of the first millennium BCE, perhaps the most significant was the rise of "New Poetry" in the vernacular during the early twentieth century. New Poetry was not just a new form but a whole new language for poetry, using the vernacular rather than the more compact classical language. Yet New Poetry grew up alongside classical poetry rather than replacing it, and poets in the Chinese-speaking world have continued to write classical poems to represent their feelings or record their thoughts. For writers of scholarly bent, classical verse has often remained a richer and more finely textured medium of expression than vernacular poetry. Writers of classical verse still retain access to the vast lexicon of imagery and symbolism, not to mention the distinct palette of emotional hues, of the earlier tradition.

On the other hand, while vernacular poetry engages actively with modern life and global culture, classical verse tends to do so only implicitly or indirectly. This is not just a matter of the vocabulary of the classical language or the constraints of the old forms. The very significance of the classical forms lies in their complex relations to Chinese history, as when recalling a phrase that was used by some long-ago emperor to lament the loss of his throne, the poet imbues his work with a dual resonance linked both to that historical moment and to his present condition. Many modern writers have taken the reasonable view that there is no way for this kind of classical form to deal with the feelings and experiences of modern Chinese. At the same time, though, some of the finest practitioners of classical verse have demonstrated that, in spite of significant limitations, it can remain a powerful medium of expression even in the globalized and technological culture of today. When it comes to the inner experience of the Chinese writer today, there are certain gradations of

---

1. 選堂其詩，不啻二十世紀中國最重要的文化招魂曲之一. From Hu's preface to *Xuantang shici lungao* (p. 6).

feeling and nostalgia that remain difficult to convey in New Poetry, just as the intimate details of modern life are not easily described in classical verse.

Jao Tsung-i 饒宗頤 (in Pinyin, Rao Zongyi) has put these propositions to the test, as much as any modern writer, in his classical Chinese verses. A brilliant scholar with a unique mastery of classical Chinese civilization, Jao has demonstrated the possibility of using the old forms and arts in context of a modern life. Privately educated by his father, Jao was steeped in classical poetry from a young age and has continued to write it throughout his life, adapting traditional forms in order to respond to his experiences in a changing China and an interconnected world. Jao has always attempted to balance both the creative practice and formal study of traditional Chinese culture. As a prolific scholar, he has made original contributions to the study of Chinese history, religion, literature, art, paleography, philosophy, and other fields; as a creative artist, he is also distinguished as painter and calligrapher, and as a master of the *qin* (a seven-stringed musical instrument resembling the zither). These poems are one of many expressive means by which Jao has sought to reinterpret and revive the traditions of Chinese culture in which he was immersed from childhood.

Biographical Sketch

Jao was born in 1917 in Chao'an 潮安, near the city of Chaozhou 潮州, located on the eastern tip of Guangdong province bordering on Fujian. The Jao family had been successful merchants in Chaozhou for generations, and Jao was educated entirely privately. The family home possessed a rarified atmosphere of scholarship and culture that was an education in itself. Jao's father Jao O 饒鍔 (1891–1932) was a devoted bibliophile whose vast library provided a fertile ground for his son's autodidacticism. Jao O was also a serious scholar, whose projects included a bibliography of Chaozhou. Though his father was not able to complete it in his own lifetime, Jao continued the project, and the *Catalogue of Arts and Letters of Chaozhou* (*Chaozhou yiwenzhi* 潮州藝文志) was one of his first publications, published in 1937 in the *Lingnan xuebao*. Jao also began writing poetry seriously at the age of twelve.[2] Little of his juvenilia survives, with the exception of a memorable poem he composed at sixteen.[3]

From 1935 to 1937, Jao was involved in compiling historical sources at Sun Yat-sen University. He then stayed at Sun Yat-sen University as a researcher at the invitation of Zhan Antai 詹安泰 (1902–1967), but after the fall of Guangzhou to the Japanese in late 1938, the university moved west to Yunnan province. Jao planned to rejoin the university, but en route stopped in Hong Kong, where illness prevented him from continuing west. In Hong Kong he met a number of important scholars who had also taken refuge there. From

---

2. See preface to the "Cheung Chau Collection," *Wenji* 462.
3. "On the Night-Blooming Kaḍupul," see Section III.

1939 to 1941 he was engaged in scholarly projects in Hong Kong, including working with Wang Yunwu 王雲五 (1888–1979) on the compilation of a dictionary. He also helped Ye Gongchuo 葉恭綽 (1881–1968) edit a compilation of Qing dynasty *ci* lyrics.[4] The *ci* has remained one of Jao's major interests throughout his life. His studies in the bibliography of *ci* from the Song through Qing have been highly influential, as well as inspiring some of his own finest poems.

Hong Kong only remained a place of refuge until December 8, 1941, when the Japanese invaded simultaneously with the surprise attack on Pearl Harbor. From 1943 to 1945 Jao taught at the Special Academy of Classical Studies in Wuxi (Wuxi guoxue zhuanxiu xuexiao 無錫國學專修學校), a school that trained many important twentieth-century scholars. During the Japanese occupation the school had relocated from Wuxi in Jiangsu to Guangxi province. Jao's exposure to life in rural Guangxi made a powerful impression on him, and many of Jao's valuable early poems date to this period, where he wrote under the dual impetus of wartime hardship and pastoral inspiration.

In 1946 Jao published his first major independent contribution to scholarship, the *Investigation of Geography in the Chuci* (*Chuci dili kao* 楚辭地理考).[5] This study already shows the rigorous critical approach to ancient texts, illuminating their background and sources, that exemplifies Jao's scholarship. This approach is complemented at a more intuitive level in Jao's original poetry by his distinctive adaptation of lines from the same classic anthology, the *Chuci*. Jao's more scholarly and formal interests interweave, throughout his life, with his many-sided artistic expression.

From 1946 to 1948 Jao was a professor at South China University in Shantou 汕頭, Guangdong. In 1949, with the founding of the People's Republic of China (PRC), Jao came to Hong Kong, and in 1952 began teaching at the University of Hong Kong, where he stayed until 1968. In that year he joined the faculty of the National University of Singapore, where he remained until 1973. During this period he also spent a year visiting at Yale (1970–1971). In 1973 he moved to the Chinese University of Hong Kong, and since then he has resided primarily in Hong Kong, though he also traveled extensively, as reflected in the poems below. Though Jao nominally retired in 1978, he has remained extremely active in scholarly, literary, and artistic endeavors since then. In recent years he has become a celebrity in Hong Kong and throughout China, and is seen as the personification of traditional culture in Hong Kong. The writer Yu Qiuyu 余秋雨 famously remarked that, but for the presence of Jao, Hong Kong would be a "cultural desert."

Throughout his career Jao traveled extensively, throughout Asia, Europe, and North America. His visits to India were perhaps the most important for his intellectual development. Jao is extremely rare among scholars of traditional China in having mastered Sanskrit. He is the author of important academic studies in the transmission of Buddhism and Indian culture to China, but perhaps more importantly, his view of life is profoundly influ-

---

4. Ye wrote the calligraphy for the cover of Jao's first poetry collection, the *Yaoshan shicao*.
5. See *Rao Zongyi ershi shiji xueshu wenji*, vol. 16.

enced by Indian Buddhism. Jao has practiced yoga for decades, and his poetry is full of references to the wisdom and serenity found in Indian culture. His knowledge of central Asia extends beyond Sanskrit to other ancient languages, allowing him to complete the first Chinese translation of the Babylonian creation epic *Enûma Eliš* (*Jindong kaipi shishi* 近東開闢史詩).

For the most part, Jao's scholarly work has focused on China itself. Some of his most important work has been on the ancient Chinese script. For instance, his classic study of oracle bone inscriptions, *Yindai zhenbu renwu tongkao* 殷代貞卜人物通考 (Comprehensive investigation of Yin dynasty diviners), was recognized by the Prix Stanislas Julien in 1962. In an important essay from 1982, he argued for a "threefold method of gathering evidence" (*sanchong zhengju fa* 三重證據法) in research on ancient China, supplementing Wang Guowei's twofold method of archaeological data and textual sources with a third, oracle bone writings.[6] In his scholarship Jao has sought consistently to take into account all the relevant evidence, regardless of its form or original language.

Jao has also argued for a broad conception of Chinese studies, recommending that the term Guoxue 國學 (literally "National Studies") be replaced by *Huaxue* 華學 ("Studies of Hua," i.e., of Chinese civilization broadly speaking). *Huaxue* is more historically accurate than Guoxue, as Chinese culture has never been confined to a single state or formed solely by the Han people, but has always been formed in interaction with other peoples throughout Asia and the world. The influence of Indian Buddhism is the most remarkable case of foreign influence, and an area to which Jao has long devoted special attention. The term *Huaxue* is especially appropriate for the twenty-first-century context, when the diaspora of the Han people, along with their language and culture, has long since spread to nearly every country of the world. Even if the precise term never achieves general popularity, the inclusive spirit behind the designation deserves our admiration.

One of the special features of Jao's work, though with many parallels in Chinese history, is his dual identity as scholar and poet. This identity is reflected in one of his pen names, Hsüan-t'ang 選堂, which means "Hall of the *Wen xuan* [the great sixth-century anthology of literature in various genres]."[7] Jao has made a revealing comment about his own view of the interrelationship of these activities. The painter Qi Baishi 齊白石 (1863–1957) once wrote, "Poetry is the residue left over from sleep; painting the residue of craft; longevity the residue of aeons. These are Baishi's three residues."[8] Jao playfully varied that sentiment, saying: "But for me, long and short verses [*ci*] are the residue of dreams; the strings of the qin are the residue of sorrow; and philology is the residue of conversation's

---

6. "Tan sanchong zhengju fa" 談三重證據法, rpt. *Rao Zongyi ershi shiji xueshu wenji* 1:12–16.

7. This pen name places Jao alongside the four masters of oracle bone studies in the early twentieth century, all of whom had scholarly pen names including the word "Hall" (*tang* 堂). According to Jao, though, it has two other layers of significance. See *Wenxue yu shenming* 149.

8. 詩者、睡之餘；畫者、工之餘；壽者、劫之餘，此白石三餘也。

spittle. These are Hsüan-t'ang's three residues."[9] In this remark he suggests how psychological experiences, dreams and sorrows, are the inspiration for his artistic production, while his scholarship is more like a form of conversation with friends or fellow scholars. His modest description of his scholarship as what is left over from "spittle" of conversation does not really do justice to the twenty volumes of his collected works, but the assertion of how creative and scholarly work interrelate is essential for understanding either dimension of Jao's achievement.

Though Jao has traveled throughout Europe, and has a number of memorable poems on cultural sites that are translated in this volume, perhaps his most memorable visit was in the company of the great Swiss sinologist Paul Demiéville (1894–1979), with whom he also collaborated on a study and translation of the songs preserved in Dunhuang manuscripts. Jao was visiting Paris in 1966 when Demiéville took him on a tour of the Swiss Alps in August of that year. As Demiéville tells it, while they were climbing through the mountains, Jao would often become entirely silent for a period of time, during which he was composing poems in his head. By the end of the journey, he had accumulated a series of quatrains which he collected as the "Poems from the Black Lake" (Heihu ji 黑湖集). Demiéville in turn translated these into elegant French, and the result forms a lovely volume that is a testament to the friendship of the two great scholars.[10]

Jao spent most of his career in Hong Kong, in circumstances far more stable and hospitable to scholarship than prevailed on the mainland during the mid-twentieth century. His efforts have mostly been pursued on behalf of China's traditional literature and culture, rather than the modern forms that developed after the May Fourth movement. In those respects he was protected from the catastrophes of the Great Leap Forward and the Great Proletarian Cultural Revolution, but he was also isolated from the cultural mainstream of China. With Hong Kong's return to the PRC, however, he has been recognized increasingly as a major figure of contemporary Chinese culture. There is also a steady and growing appreciation of the traditional forms of Chinese culture, of which Jao is one of the more prominent representatives and living embodiments today. We may hope that the arc of Jao Tsung-i's life, though highly anomalous in the twentieth century, will turn out to establish a pattern for many Chinese scholars and artists in the twenty-first.

Jao as Poet

Jao's classical Chinese writings were published privately at first, but over the past few decades they have been compiled and republished numerous times. The compilations are

---

9. 余則以長短句為夢之餘，琴絲為悲之餘，考證為唾之餘，此選堂之三餘也 (*Wenji* 646). "Spittle" is used as metonymy for conversation or literary composition, beginning with *Zhuangzi* 31.1026.

10. Published as *Poèmes du lac noir*.

mostly thematic, like his writings from Yaoshan during the Japanese occupation, *Draft Poems from Yaoshan* (*Yaoshan shicao* 瑤山詩草), or from his journey to India, "The Land of the Buddha" (Foguo ji 佛國集).[11] They have also been compiled, as Jao's fame has grown, under various of his pen names. These include Hsüan-t'ang, but also Gu'an 固庵, "Studio of Steadfastness," and Qinghui 清暉, "Pure Light." Chinese scholars have begun to devote considerable attention to these literary compositions, writing specialized studies of his work. This attention is a deserved tribute to the passion and eloquence of these writings. Jao composes classical Chinese with a facility and precision that make it a potent medium of expression for searching philosophical reflections, vivid depictions of natural scenes, and moving lamentations on historical tragedy. He combines an impeccable command of the Chinese tradition with wide-ranging erudition in other languages and cultures. While his poetic diction reworks that of Xie Lingyun 謝靈運 (385–433) or Li Shangyin 李商隱 (813–858), his allusions extend beyond the classical tradition to take in Plato or Nietzsche, and the topics of his poems range from familiar ones like the Double Ninth festival to novel subjects like the Grand Canyon or Taj Mahal.

The importance of Jao's scholarship on Chinese script, literature, philosophy, Buddhism, and countless other topics has long been recognized internationally, but his literary works have received little attention in the West. This neglect is due in part to a problem of classification. Because of the special nature of China's dramatic transition into the twentieth century, the break between the "premodern" and "modern" is often seen as a fundamental gap between scholarly disciplines. The abrupt termination of Manchu rule in 1911 was followed in 1919 by the May Fourth movement, which revolutionized the Chinese language itself, a decade of radical transformation in both politics and culture. Even the Chinese written language was transformed, with a new vernacular style being established as the norm for both prose and poetry. Since he eschewed the vernacular and wrote in the "classical" language, Jao is hard to place within the conventional narrative of modern Chinese literature. Confronting the writings of Jao Tsung-i, we certainly cannot identify an author born in 1917 as pre-twentieth century; but it is equally hard to read poetry in forms one or two millennia old as "modern." For this reason Jao's poems, like the work of countless contemporaries throughout the Chinese-speaking world, have generally been overlooked in accounts of modern literature. The conceptual division between modern and imperial China has resulted in neglect of major portions of China's twentieth-century culture.

Fortunately, the twenty-first century has seen a burgeoning interest in post-1919 classical poetry. One valuable effort toward a reappraisal is Tian Xiaofei's recent essay presenting an "Alternative History of Modern Chinese Poetry."[12] Tian selects three modern

---

11. Both are included in *Wenji* (pp. 533–554 and 349–365, respectively).

12. The full title is "Muffled Dialect Spoken by Green Fruit: An Alternative History of Modern Chinese Poetry." See also the studies by von Kowallis, *The Lyrical Lu Xun* and *The Subtle Revolution*. Since completing this manuscript I have also obtained the recent monograph by Wu Shengqing,

writers of classical verse: Huang Zunxian 黃遵憲 (1848–1905), Nie Gannu 聶紺弩 (1903–1986), and Internet poet Lizilizilizi 李子梨子栗子 (1964–). Tian skillfully shows how closely the classical verse of these poets engages with China's historical transformations in the twentieth century. Huang Zunxian writes of his experiences as a diplomat in Europe and Japan, leading China's initial efforts to join the world powers; Nie Gannu writes ironically of the Cultural Revolution and the intellectual restrictions imposed by the Communist Party; and Lizilizilizi publishes directly on the Internet and establishes utterly new frontiers for classical Chinese verse. Tian's essay confirms the relevance of classical verse for any full recounting of the history of modern Chinese poetry: a history in which Jao Tsung-i may also find a permanent place.

Jao's collected works do include a single poem in modern Chinese *vers libre*,[13] but otherwise he has written entirely in classical verse forms, and even much of his published prose is in more or less classical style. In their contents, though, these works range over a vast swathe of both the modern world and Chinese tradition. There is a great deal of continuity between the classical and modern written languages, and much of Jao's writing is accessible to any educated Chinese reader. Moreover, he frequently writes about his own emotions or places he has visited, limning circumstances that could occur only in modern times. Yet Jao's poems are actively engaged with the imperial past, their densely allusive style frequently referring to different source in every single line.[14]

Sometimes Jao's engagement with the poetic tradition goes beyond simple allusions to structure an entire poem or series of poems. For instance, one of Jao's favorite techniques is to follow the rhymes of an earlier poet. This was a well-established practice in China since the Song dynasty, and is known as *he* 和, "matching the rhymes." Jao frequently engaged in poetic conversations with other scholars and poets, his interlocutors including not just other Hong Kong residents, but Chinese writers around the world, and even several Japanese sinologists. In many of these exchanges Jao uses the rhymes of a friend's poem to respond to that poem, or vice versa. But the practice is not limited to living poets; many of Jao's compositions employ the rhymes of ancient poets as well. In considering the meaning of this practice, we should recall Arthur Henry Hallam's (1811–1833) stimulating maxim: "Rhyme has been said to contain in itself a constant appeal to memory and hope."[15]

Modern Archaics, which provides valuable new insights into the achievements of classical poetry in the early twentieth century.

13. *Wenji* 766–769.

14. Some classical poets in the nineteenth and twentieth centuries have also employed a more straightforward diction in their classical poetry. For examples in late Qing verse, see Schmidt, *Within the Human Realm: The Poet Zheng Zhen (1806–1864)*; and also Chaves, *The Columbia Book of Later Chinese Poetry*, e.g., the poems of Liu E 劉鶚 (1857–1909) (pp. 466–475).

15. "Oration on the Influence of Italian Works of the Imagination on the Same Class of Compositions in England," in *Remains in Verse and Prose of Arthur Henry Hallam: With a Preface and a Memoir*, 125.

In a century of turmoil, when the treasures of Chinese culture were overlooked or willfully destroyed, Jao found in his engagement with earlier poetry not just memory but also hope.

Apart from matching rhymes, Jao also refers throughout his work to poems from the Chinese tradition, and even poems from other traditions. These citations in general are not quoted directly from the primary sources, but are copied instead from Jao's capacious mind. For instance, Jao has written a poem entitled "Reading the Poetry of Rimbaud."[16] The poem refers to a number of Arthur Rimbaud's (1854–1891) poems, so the reader might at first imagine that Jao has composed it while simultaneously scanning a volume of Rimbaud's works. In fact, a miscitation reveals that his approach was slightly different. In a note to the poem, Jao quotes a line from Baudelaire's "Le Voyage": "Au fond de l'Inconnu pour trouver du nouveau!" but misattributes it to Rimbaud. This is hardly the kind of mistake one could make while copying out selections from a volume of Rimbaud. It could only be a lapse of memory by a poet who, in his spare time, has mastered some of nineteenth-century French verse. Jao must be quoting Rimbaud directly from memory, as is his practice with Chinese texts.

Jao's matching poems provide a sense of the community among Sinophone scholars in the twentieth century, extending far beyond national boundaries and political divisions. Jao exchanges poems with fellow scholars, writers, and artists throughout the Chinese-speaking diaspora, extending from Singapore to Paris. Within the grand enterprise of traditional Chinese civilization, he also treats as friends and colleagues poets of the distant past. Although Jao stands apart from many of his contemporaries and the practice of modern vernacular poetry, then, his poems never come across as solipsistic. He is always writing as one of a visionary corps, reiterating and reimagining the ideals of his tradition.

The poems sometimes have a hermetic quality, distantly reminiscent of Stefan George or Rimbaud himself. But Jao was heavily influenced by the style of late Qing poets, who were striving to deploy classical forms to new expressive ends.[17] Through veils of allusion, imagery, and ellipsis, Jao is deeply concerned with the contemporary geopolitical situation, particularly the fate of the Chinese people. His "Essay on Horse Manure" stands with the antiwar literature of the twentieth century as a unique protest against man's inhumanity to man. His poems of the sixties and seventies are collectively a remarkable response to the traumas of the Great Proletarian Cultural Revolution on the mainland. Jao's poems form a remarkable record of the inner thoughts and reflections of a superbly talented Chinese man of letters. They track his emotional states and intellectual recollections from youth to old age, across continents and oceans. Even apart from their substantial literary value, they have an independent kind of status as the psychological record of a unique mind.

Jao is not primarily a political poet, and for his most compelling achievements we should probably look to his lyrics of personal reflection, particularly the philosophical

---

16. Included in Section II.
17. On this background see von Kowallis, *The Subtle Revolution*.

works on topics like "Self" and "Spirit." Though writing within the traditional constraints of the *ci* (not only metrically and prosodically but in terms of imagery and diction as well), Jao finds in this traditional literary form a kind of objective correlative to his ineffable thoughts and feelings. In these poems Jao writes with a subjective, elliptical density, in which disparate images cohere in an intuitive, associative manner. To return to the dichotomy of the "modern" and "traditional," they are fully "modern," in the Western conception of modern poetry that was set forth by Ezra Pound, himself under the influence of traditional Chinese poetry. For Pound it was the restrained expression of emotion through telling physical details, set forth paratactically without enjambment, that made Chinese poetry the epitome of imagistic poetry, through which he aimed to make a revolution in contemporary literature.[18] Yet the traditional forms of Chinese poetry, which remain popular even today and were so productive in their modernist transposition, have long been treated with condescension by sinologists as historical artifacts irrelevant to the modern world. In fact Jao's poetry is most modern when most fully realizing ideals of allusive subjectivity and implicit symbolism that are classically Chinese: one of those ironic reversals of which our literary histories, as our lives, are made.

Overview of Genres and Sources

This selection encompasses examples of Jao's writings in various genres of Chinese poetry: *shi* 詩, *ci* 詞, *fu* 賦, etc. Here I provide a brief overview of these forms, as well as the major writers who figure as sources or influences for Jao.[19]

Shi poetry is the most basic form of Chinese poetry. With his *shi* poems, Jao engages in dialogue not just with his own contemporaries, but also with historical poets from Ruan Ji 阮籍 (210–263) to Su Shi 蘇軾 (1037–1101). *Shi* poems have a fixed number of syllables per line, generally either five characters long (pentasyllabic) or seven characters long (heptasyllabic). *Shi* poetry can also be classified as either "ancient-style" or "regulated." Ancient-style verse is more flexible, lacking tonal regulations, while regulated verse has relatively strict tonal patterns and also requires parallelism in some couplets. Jao writes in all the main forms of the *shi*, but his favorite is probably "ancient-style pentasyllabic verse" (*wu gu* 五古).

The poets who exert the most obvious influence on Jao's *shi* poetry include three outstanding poets of the early medieval period: Ruan Ji 阮籍 (210–263), Tao Yuanming 陶淵明 (365–427), and Xie Lingyun 謝靈運 (385–433); the distinctive voices of Li Shangyin 李商隱 (813–858) and Li He 李賀 (790–816) from the late Tang era; and finally Su Shi

---

18. On this curious history see Yip, *Ezra Pound's Cathay*.

19. Two helpful books that introduce the main genres and key texts are Owen, *An Anthology of Chinese Literature: Beginnings to 1911*, and Cai Zong-qi, ed., *How to Read Chinese Poetry: A Guided Anthology*.

蘇軾 (1037–1101), the Northern Song dynasty polymath. Jao also alludes to other major poets who shaped the poetic tradition, such as Du Fu 杜甫 (712–770), but the group named above seems to have a special significance for Jao beyond their literary–historical importance per se. In particular, he frequently matches the rhymes of all these poets. The exception that proves the rule is Jao's series of poems matching the rhymes of Du Fu's classic "Autumn Meditations." In his preface to these poems Jao concedes that he has failed to imitate Du Fu's style, instead tending against his own will toward that of Li Shangyin.

Ruan Ji was one of the group of eccentrics and free spirits known as the "Seven Worthies of the Bamboo Grove."[20] He is a poet of particularly philosophical bent, mingling meditations on mortality and fate with enigmatic images of melancholy and dread. Jao's special fondness for Ruan is reflected in his remarkable "Cheung Chau Collection" matching the rhymes of all Ruan's eighty-two pentasyllabic poems. Tao Yuanming, even more than Ruan Ji, has been a powerful role model for Chinese literati throughout the past millennium.[21] He is particularly renowned for renouncing official service and retiring to his farm. Xie Lingyun, scion of an extremely influential and wealthy family, led a less admired life, but wrote exquisite poems on his excursions through the mountains and rivers around his personal estate. He often ends these poems with a "metaphysical tail," a dry philosophical conclusion uneasily integrated with the remainder of the poem. Though this feature has been criticized by later readers, Jao sometimes imitates it.

Li Shangyin and Li He are representative of the new poetics of the late Tang dynasty.[22] Li He's most memorable and characteristic pieces take up either supernatural or historical topics.[23] For instance, in a poem on the bronze camels of Luoyang, he adopts the point of view of the camels themselves, weeping as they observe the turmoil of war and the fall of dynasties.[24] His unconventional perspectives and fondness for the otherworldly have not always been well-received by Chinese readers, but give him an appealingly modern tone. Much the same is true, for different reasons, of Li Shangyin's densely allusive poetry. Li's style occasionally approaches that of a Verlaine or Rilke, one complex image following the next with only a vague association of mood to link them. Another striking feature of Li Shangyin's poetry is his enigmatic "Untitled" pieces, which have been the subject of ongoing debate ever since their debut. Because the title refrains from identifying the subject matter, and the content consists largely of evocative but disconnected images and allusions, the reader is forced to speculate as to whether the poet is referring to some love af-

---

20. For Ruan's poetry see Holzman, *Poetry and Politics*.

21. Although, curiously, Tao was not as celebrated in the centuries immediately after his death. For Tao's poems see Hightower, *The Poetry of T'ao Ch'ien*.

22. For a useful overview and selection, see Graham, *Poems of the Late T'ang*; a more detailed study of the mid-ninth century is Owen, *The Late Tang*.

23. The former is reflected in the title of J.D. Frodsham's translation: *Goddesses, Ghosts, and Demons: The Collected Poems of Li He (790–816)*.

24. See Frodsham, *Goddesses, Ghosts and Demons*, 142.

fair, or political complaint, or something else altogether. Jao seems to find this obscure mode quite appealing and useful. His affinity for Ruan Ji and Li Shangyin is particularly noticeable during the tense years of the Great Proletarian Cultural Revolution.

Finally one cannot ignore Jao's appreciation for Su Shi, the enormously prolific and protean polymath of the Northern Song dynasty.[25] Su Shi, who was also accomplished in music, art, and calligraphy, and was actively involved in the great political debates of his time as well, is in many ways a model for Jao as renaissance man (with the exception that scholars no longer have much opportunity to affect government policies). Su was a great and original writer in all the major genres of Chinese poetry, but Jao seems to devote less attention to his *ci*, still very popular today, and more to his *shi* poetry, whose rhymes he frequently matches. Su's *shi* poems often have a relaxed, occasional quality, commenting freely on his current situation or observing the scene around him. Jao seems to find this precedent particularly useful for writing about his own travels, although Jao's work does not achieve quite the same sense of spontaneous delight so that is so characteristic in Su Shi.

The *ci* or "song lyric" developed during the Tang dynasty, though most of the major *ci* writers appeared only in the succeeding Song dynasty. These were originally the lyrics to actual songs, and every *ci* is written to a "tune pattern." Thus *ci* poems in this volume can easily be distinguished by the titles "To the Tune of …" . I have translated these titles because they are extremely colorful and suggestive, even though they generally lack any direct connection to the content of a new lyric. The formatting of these poems is also distinctive, with indentations to suggest their distinctive prosody, usually heterometric and thus apparently irregular, but in fact quite strictly following the designated tune pattern. Though the original tunes have mostly been lost, writers use the tune patterns as literary forms, shaping the line length, tones, and rhyme schemes of their compositions. Jao's scholarship on the texts of lyrics from the past is one of his outstanding achievements. His lyrics frequently allude to classic lyrics from the Song dynasty, but also to other major lyrics from throughout the tradition, particularly certain Qing lyricists. In this genre as well, Jao is fond of matching the rhymes both of famous poems from the past, and of his contemporaries.

The *ci* lyric has the strictest constraints of the literary forms that Jao has used. The tune pattern itself imposes constraints, but the *ci* tradition also requires that a poem follow other conventions regarding content, diction, and syntax. One important convention regards the content and symbolism of the song lyric. These are very often drawn from the language of the courtesan or singing girl. Early writers of *ci* were often composing songs to be performed not by themselves, but by professional singing girls, and *ci* often allude to this practice. Another popular category of *ci* topics is floral imagery, such as Jao's beloved plum blossom. This category is closely related to the previous one through the traditional

---

25. See the detailed study by Ronald Egan, *Word, Image, and Deed in the Life of Su Shi*, which ranges from Su's religious and political interests to his prose and poetic compositions. Michael Fuller's *The Road to East Slope* is a more focused treatment of the development of Su's poetic style.

analogy between pretty flowers and pretty women. These conventions would seem to mean that the *ci* are somewhat inappropriate for Jao to use in writing of his own life of scholarship and foreign travel. In fact, though, like great *ci* writers of the past, Jao also reworks the conventions to convey his feeling, state of mind, and even more philosophical reflections on the self or the soul.[26] Even though the form involves the strictest constraints on literary expression, Jao finds in it the vehicle of some of his most revealingly personal writing.

The two *ci* writers cited most frequently by Jao are Zhou Bangyan 周邦彥 (1056–1121) and Jiang Kui 姜夔 (ca. 1155–ca. 1235). These are two of the *ci* poets most responsible for using the *ci* form to create an almost abstract world of memory and melancholy. Zhou Bangyan was particularly important as an innovator: according to James J.Y. Liu, "In his hands the lyric reached new heights of subtlety and sophistication both in its modes of sensibility and in its modes of expression."[27] Zhou is also known for his skillful adaptations of Tang verses, a feature that Jao studied closely. Indeed Jao regards Zhou's *ci* so highly that he has an entire book of *ci* entitled the "Emulating Zhou Collection" (Xi Zhou ji 睎周集).[28] Jiang Kui writes in a style similar to that of Zhou, focusing on memory and mood, as opposed to the more swashbuckling style of his contemporary Xin Qiji 辛棄疾 (1140–1207), in whom Jao shows relatively little interest. Jiang Kui is particularly famous for his *yongwu* poems "on things," which have a designated topic like the plum blossom, and create some kind of mood around that object rather than merely attempting to describe it explicitly. It is perhaps in the *ci* form that Jao is most original, and the task of tracing his poetic sources the least fruitful. This is particularly the case for his so-called metaphysical *ci*, of which several have been selected for this volume.[29]

Jao remarked on his own practice of *ci* composition, in the postface to the "Emulating Zhou Collection" written in March 1971 while visiting New Haven:[30]

> Writing *ci* to match the rhymes of earlier works, one must be careful not to become mired in the superficial meaning of the verses. Instead one ought to proceed by *qi* energy alone, leaping, shifting, flowing, and turning, hoping to attain a full-formed separate world. This is what I most hope to achieve, though I may not always succeed. ... For creativity is in the sense and in the brushstroke [choice of words], but

---

26. In fact *ci* have always been capable of being used as the vehicle of literary, personal, and philosophical subtleties. On their philosophical implications see, e.g., Brook Ziporyn's "Temporal Paradoxes: Intersections of Time Present and Time Past in the Song *ci*."

27. Liu, *Major Lyricists of the Northern Sung*, 161.

28. *Wenji* 604–644.

29. See Jao's postface to volume one of the "Emulating Zhou Collection," *Wenji* 625, and also the essay by Lam Lap, "Xuantang xingshang ci zhi wo jian."

30. *Wenji* 643.

not in the form. One would need grandiose pretension to claim to be able to produce something novel while lacking any particular brushstroke that is one's own.

In other words, Jao borrows the forms of earlier poets, but still hopes to demonstrate originality in his particular phrasings and new sentiments.

The *fu* is a particularly difficult form to define.[31] *Fu* has been translated as "rhapsody" or "poetic exposition," but this translator here renders it as "essay," short for "verse essay," in the sense of Pope's "Essay on Man." In the Han dynasty the *fu* was primarily a court composition, often eulogizing the sovereign in splendidly ornate language. But already in the Han, and increasingly during the succeeding dynasties, the *fu* also took various other forms, including that of a personal meditation on some topic at hand. Jao's best *fu* belong to this type and were written during the Japanese occupation. Two of these are included in this volume: the "Essay on Horse Manure" and "Essay on White Clouds." These are important works of wartime literature that deserve at least a footnote in histories of modern Chinese literature. I also include three more playful later works: the "Essay on Crabs," "Essay on Cloudgazing," and *fu*-like "Encomium for the Mawangdui Silk Manuscript." The *fu* lack the delicate charm of Jao's *ci* lyrics, but they are the compositions in his oeuvre that best exemplify Tian Xiaofei's thesis that classical poetry in modern times has developed in tandem with major historical events.

Conventions of This Translation

This book aims to be a suggestive selection of Jao's works that will introduce him to English-speaking readers. Though I have drawn on poems from a variety of genres and subjects, I have not tried to make the selection comprehensive. In general I have tried to select pieces that reflect Jao's most striking artistic successes. In the case of the *ci* I have been aided by the anthology *Ershi shiji shi da jia ci xuan*, which selects ten of Jao's *ci* as highlights of twentieth-century lyrical art, and I have translated all these pieces.

Regarding the style and method of the translation, I have in general attempted to remain close to the original texts, translating line by line to preserve the precise structure of syntax and imagery in the original poems. Other methods would also be appropriate for translating Jao's poems. In particular, it would have been possible to be more free and aim primarily to reflect the emotion and gist of the poems. But for the first translation into English, the primary desideratum is to get into English the precise formulations of Jao's original works. This is particularly true as his poems are so luxuriantly laden in allusion to Chinese culture. In many lines, the paraphrasable content has little to do with the variety of connotations suggested by the specific formulation. The translation of Jao's poetry has

---

31. For an overview of the early development of the *fu*, see Knechtges, *The Han Rhapsody*.

to begin with the struggle for accuracy, with preliminary "raids on the inarticulate." Perhaps at some future occasion when more of the sources of Jao's work—from the entire Chinese poetic tradition—have been translated, it will be possible to prepare a more free and fluent translation relying less upon approximation of other Chinese sources for which there are not yet adequate English versions.

At the same time, there are rewards for fidelity to the specific diction, structure, and syntax of Jao's poems. Jao's scholarly and literary modus operandi is one of almost superhuman precision. Never content with vague generalizations, Jao's oeuvre is devoted to singular texts, writers, and historical moments, as suggested in his lifelong attention to epigraphy. He never overlooks the precise words used to express a thought, to the extent of paying close attention to the physical contours of the Chinese characters. In translating Jao's poetry, I have had in mind Nabokov's criticism of reviewers who praise a translation because "easy platitudes have replaced in it the intricacies of which he is unaware."[32] This translation aims to read clearly but also to reproduce some of the intricacies of the original poems.

The poems are grouped into categories that suggest some of the major themes and consistent interests of Jao's poems. Section I is devoted to some of Jao's earliest surviving poems, dated to the years of Japanese occupation, some of which are very serious and others of which are more whimsical depictions of life in Yaoshan 瑤山 (northern Guangdong province), where Jao had temporarily taken refuge. The next two sections, II and III, include a variety of poems on either Euro-American (Western Parallels) or Asian (Eastern Visions) topics. The following three sections (IV–VI) include a variety of poems of personal reflection in downcast moods, whether out of concern for the state of mainland China in the 1960s or for other reasons generally not stated explicitly in the poems. These include two sets of poems matching the rhymes of earlier poets (Du Fu and Tao Yuanming). The next four sections (VII–X) include poems on artistic, literary, or scholarly themes. Finally the book concludes with a section of "dreams," presenting some of Jao's most imaginative and philosophical poems.

Poems are selected from various genres to represent the range of Jao's work, including the *fu* (rendered here as "essay"), *shi* poems, and *ci* lyrics. I have provided rough translations titles for the tune patterns, which substitute for titles in the case of *ci*. The *ci* translated here comprise two stanzas, and the break between stanzas is marked by a line of asterisks.

One striking aspect of all Jao's poetry is a paraliterary element: apart from all the allusions to past literature, his writings also overflow with learned prefaces, postfaces, footnotes, subtitles. With regret, I have not always included these elements here, since together with the annotations I have provided to help the reader in making sense of the translations, they might overburden the reader. I have for the most part translated the prefaces,

---

32. Preface to Pushkin, *Eugene Onegin*, ix.

however, which illustrate Jao's unique charm of combining erudition, elegance, and feeling, and are often small masterpieces of classical prose in their own right. Here as elsewhere Jao is continuing the great tradition of literati writing. It has long been the practice of *ci* lyric writers, in particular, to write exquisite prefaces contextualizing their works. As Shuen-fu Lin has written, "A title or preface allows the poet to specify a song as belonging or having relation to something, be it a person, thing, event, or situation, in the *lebenswelt* of the poet."[33]

Jao's use of earlier poetry (his "intertextuality") is pervasive, and I have not attempted to identify all allusions, quotations, or parallels in the notes. I have also not quoted the poems whose rhymes Jao is often matching. Frequently Jao is using these earlier poems as a kind of reference point in the background, but his own poem may veer in a different direction, using similar literary means to different expressive ends. Whether the source material is essential to interpretation of any particular piece is open to debate and further investigation, though it is certainly true that Jao expects any reader to be familiar with the bulk of his sources. The interested reader could consult the volumes of translations and studies by Frodsham, Watson, Lin, Liu, etc. that are listed in the bibliography, to gain a sense of the tradition that lies in the background of Jao's poems. The *fu* are less accessible, and the full poetic tradition that Jao has in mind extends beyond the Tang-Song giants up through late imperial times, and then right up through the twentieth century to the present. Their full scope could only be described by an entire encyclopedia of Chinese tradition. Nonetheless, many of the key sources are available in excellent English translations. When such are available, I have provided citations to these in my notes, although I have often modified the translations from these sources to conform with my own versions of Jao's poems. In many cases, where English translations are not accessible or convenient, I have only cited the original Chinese texts. Legge's excellent translations of the classics, for instance, have become inconvenient for laymen due to changes in romanization and other technical matters.

In spite of the limitations of Western scholarship, though, it should be possible for all readers of discernment to appreciate Jao's poems, which are full not only of learning and erudition, but also of sadness, wit, beauty, and dreams.

---

33. Lin, *The Transformation of the Chinese Lyric Tradition*, 65.

I

Taking Refuge

As Jao was forced into flight by the Japanese occupation of Hong Kong in 1941, he took refuge in the Yaoshan 瑤山 *and Beiliu* 北流 *mountain region in Guangxi province. In 1945 he compiled the poems written at these places into the "Yao Mountain Collection." In the preface to the collection he explains the context of their composition:*[1]

> Last summer when Guilin reported danger, I fled west to Mengshan. That winter the Japanese occupied Mengshan too, so I found refuge in a remote village. Entrusting my meager life to the reeds here is like that ancient hero finding sustenance with washerwomen on the strand.[2] I went up into the Yao mountains, climbing up vines ten yards long, and admiring the pomelo trees one hundred armlengths. With rainclouds filling out the entire firmament, and river deer crying out for their own kind, I seemed to encounter exactly the kind of scene that Qu Yuan and Xiaoshan had written of in their sorrowful elegies.[3] I have been forced into flight east, west, north, and south,[4] lost somewhere in a vast and dreadful realm.

For the most part, the poems in this section do not dwell on Jao's troubles, but rather describe his enjoyment and relief in the natural scenery of Guangxi. Jao explains why he has collected the poems:

---

1. *Wenji* 534.
2. Referring to a story about Han Xin 韓信 (?–196 BCE), who helped Liu Bang 劉邦 (247–195) to found the Han dynasty. See *Shi ji* 92.2609.
3. Qu Yuan is the poet and nobleman who wrote the "Li sao" on being exiled from the court of Chu. Xiaoshan of Huainan is the pen name of the author of "Summons to a Recluse," also included in the *Chuci* 楚辭 anthology.
4. Du Fu once applied this expression to himself, but originally Confucius had described himself as a wanderer in all four directions. See *Li ji zhengyi* 6.7a.

I composed these writings while under great hardship, so properly they should be tossed away and spoken of no more, but now that I have traveled to strange soils, I can no longer bear to discard them. Burning a lamp in a bamboo window I reread these poems, and it is like reviving an old dream. These writings are like a tattered broomstick, a paltry thing but mine own, so why not share them?[5]

To the Tune of "Gaoyang Terrace"[5]

I wrote this piece while a refugee during the War of Resistance. A friend kept a copy, and it is a rare remnant of my early writings, so I have recorded it here.[6]

雨濕蕪城	The ruined city drenched in rain,
鴉翻遙浦	crows turn back from the far shore
倦遊遠客驚心	and this traveler is heartbroken from wandering.
千里兵塵	The dust of war extends a thousand miles,
野風腥入羅衾	and gales drive rank air under our gauze bedcovers.
玉簫難續繁華夢	No jade flutes can sustain the splendid dream:
倚危亭	from a high pavilion I see
迢遞層陰	shadows deepening in the distance.
雁訊沉	Geese-borne messages are lost,
葉驚征魂	falling leaves startle the soul in flight,
風起騷吟	and the wind seems to stir an elegy into song.

           *   *   *

江山如此故交渺	The world in this state, old friends are far away,
又樓高天迴	just as towers are high and Heaven remote:
節往秋深	the season slips away in autumn's deepening chill.
平楚寒煙	Freezing mists rise on the wild plains,
儘多鄉思楓林	I grow homesick in maple groves.
銅駝荊棘知何世	With "bronze camels in brambles" what era is this now?[7]
舞吳鉤	Wu scimitars dance,
豈獨傷今	but we do not grieve only because of today.
意難任	It is hard to bear
霜落蕭晨	frostfall at dawn:
休去登臨	better not to climb high and look down.[8]

---

5. 高陽臺. *Wenji* 752.

6. As mentioned above, prefaces to poems printed in roman type as here are authored by Jao. Prefaces in italics, by contrast, are added by the translator.

7. Suo Jing 索靖 (239–303) had a premonition of the disaster approaching the Western Jin dynasty, and would lament by the bronze camels at the gates of Luoyang: "I will see you again amid the brambles and thorns!" See *Jin shu* 60.1648.

8. Cf. Liu Yong's "Eight Beats of a Ganzhou Song": "I cannot bear to climb high and look far" (Liu, *Major Lyricists of the Northern Sung*, 62).

Various Poems on the Double-Ninth Day[9]

The ninth day of the ninth month, or the Double Ninth, was a traditional holiday on which one would customarily ascend to a high place, drink chrysanthemum wine, and adorn oneself with dogwood branches. It was a popular occasion for poetry composition since medieval times.[10]

#1

中酒枯腸亦吐芒	Though soused in drink my famished innards still put out fresh shoots.
高秋坐惜去堂堂	At the height of autumn I only regret how long I have journeyed.
江山不負勞人意	The rivers and mountains do not disappoint a refugee's expectation,
又放頹陽到野塘	But allow the sun to retreat all the way to a country pond.

#2

菊帶霜威護短籬	Chrysanthemums, facing frost's encroachment, are guarded by a low fence;
危城清釅敵淒其	On towering walls I drink pure dark tea to calm my feeling of desperation.
山河表裏如襟帶	Mountains and rivers form surface and reverse, their folds like lapel and sash;
誰信投荒莫在斯	Who would believe that I would take refuge in such a place as this?

#3

碧澗中藏萬斛愁	Hidden within emerald streams, ten thousand bushels of woe:
浮雲偏滯古蒙州	The floating clouds have paused somewhere in old Mengzhou.[11]
亦知竹葉非無分	Since I know there may still be a portion of Bamboo Leaf wine,
難得山翁折簡留	How precious that the Mountain Hermit would write me an invitation.[12]

#4

峽裏輕雷晚自哀	Hearing light thunder in the gorges, I feel grief stir at evening.
干戈憂患鎮相催	War and pillage, dread and disaster, have harried me hither.
人間未廢登高例	The custom of climbing a high place has not yet been discarded,
且插茱萸歸去來	So I'll stick dogwood in my hair thinking of return, oh! return—[13]

---

9. 九日雜詩. *Wenji* 538.

10. This preface is added by the translator, as are all prefaces in italics. See Davis, "The Double Ninth Festival in Chinese Poetry," for texts of the most famous Tang poems on the topic.

11. Mengzhou is located in the area of modern Wuzhou 梧州 city, in eastern Guangxi near the Yaoshan mountains.

12. The Mountain Hermit is a historical personage, Shan Jian 山簡 (253–312), who was famous for his drinking.

13. As in a famous poem by Tao Yuanming, "The Return!" 歸去來兮辭. See Hightower, *The Poetry of T'ao Ch'ien*, 268–270.

#5

繭足猶能卻曲吟	Feet calloused from trudging along, I hum along my crooked way;[14]
萬山何處白雲深	Where among these ten thousand peaks are the white clouds deepest?
莫愁九日多風雨	Don't worry that there will be storms and rain on the Double Ninth;
記取壺冰一片心	Keep in your memory this heart pure as a vase of ice.[15]

---

14. This line refers to the song attributed to the madman Jie Yu in *Zhuangzi*: "I walk a crooked way—don't step on my feet." See Watson, *Zhuangzi: Basic Writings*, 62 (cf. *Zhuangzi* 4.183).

15. The expression does not refer to a heart that is cold in the sense of being unfeeling or ungrateful, but rather pure and serene. It derives from Wang Changling's 王昌齡 (ca. 698–757) famous couplet: "If my friends in Luoyang should ask about me: / I'm just a heart of ice in a jade vase." Cf. Owen, *The Great Age of Chinese Poetry*, 91.

Ballad of Yaoshan[16]

A ballad in which Jao at first complains about his rustic surroundings, but gradually finds some satisfaction in his isolation there.

薄薄瑤山酒	Yaoshan wine is weak to the taste;
日日不離口	Daily it does not stray from my mouth.
瑤女未解愁	Yaoshan girls cannot grasp what sadness is:
楚客空搔首	A Chu traveler scratches his head in futility.[17]
村村聞鴃舌	In every village all I hear is shrike-tongue speech,[18]
家家盡堙牖	And every house has windows filled with mud.
老松八千尺	The old pine is eight thousand feet high,
日傍北風吼	And daily howls in the north wind.
山花乍吐妍	All at once mountain flowers burst into bloom,
山石漸變醜	As gradually the mountain crags begin to look homely.
五里沈霧迷	A distance of five miles will disappear in the fog,
公超挾我走	As Master Transcendence leads me away.[19]
本性侶麋鹿	By nature I'm companion to the elaphure and deer,[20]
何意跨蒼狗	Why try to straddle the grizzled dogs in their flux?[21]
世亂隱佯狂	In a time of disorder you must go into hiding and feign madness,
捉襟時見肘	So poor that when you touch your collar the elbow shows.
赤足拖狐裘	Barefoot and trailing a foxskin cloak,
此趣笑誰有	Who can share in this laughter and delight?

---

16. 瑤山詠. *Wenji* 547.

17. The "Chu traveler" suggests both the ancient exile-poet-hero Qu Yuan and Jao himself.

18. "Shrike-tongue speech" refers to local dialects that are difficult to understand. See *Mengzi zhushu* 5B.5a.

19. Master Transcendence was the style name of Zhang Kai 張楷 (80–149), a recluse who practiced Daoist magical arts to create "five miles of fog." See *Hou Han shu* 36.1243.

20. The elaphure is a species of deer with unique antlers that is native to China. It is also known as "Père David's deer."

21. This is an allusion to Du Fu's "Lamentable" 可嘆: "The floating clouds in the sky look now like white robes, / Then in a moment transform into grizzled dogs." See *Du shi xiangzhu* 21.1830.

萬方聲一概	The sounds from the myriad places are all alike,
到此忘陽九	But coming here you forget the Double Ninth.
所欠花豬肉	The only thing I'm missing is marbled pork loin:
無食使人瘦	Nothing to eat can make a person thin.
行歌聳驢肩	Singing as I roam on donkey shoulders,
歸路逐牛後	On the return trip I follow behind an ox.
長嘯叫孫登	With a long whistle I summon the recluse Sun Deng,[22]
客夢落林藪	A traveler dreaming of rest in a shrouded coppice here.

Illustration 2. *Yaoshan Waterfall* (2004).

---

22. Sun Deng was a recluse familiar to Ruan Ji. "Whistling" was a Daoist breathing exercise, considerably more intense than the whistling with which we are familiar today.

Mankind Day[23]

"Mankind Day" is the Seventh Day of the New Year according to the old lunar calendar. This poem was composed at the beginning of 1945 while Jao was a refugee in Guangxi.[24]

窮陰皂白不能分	At the depth of winter white and black are indistinguishable;
誰遣春風散重雲	Who will send the spring wind to disperse the wreathed clouds?
嶺西千古斷腸地	West of Lingnan was the site of heartbreak for a thousand ages,
酒澆不下胸輪囷	No wine can purge the knottings in my breast.
僵臥松氈數人日	Lying straight on a blanket of pine I count the seventh day,
流年似鳥遄飛疾	The years passing as rapidly as birds that dart away.
仍是東西南北人	Still I remain a man divided east, west, north, south—[25]
此身歸去安能必	How can I find assurance of a return home?
萬里風波一葉舟	One little boat riding the wind and waves one thousand leagues,
青山百匝繞蒙州	The green hills hundredfold surround Mengzhou.
流離豈是長無謂	Even a refugee cannot be forever reticent,
懷古端須志窮愁	But for nostalgia's sake records his bottomless sorrow.

---

23. 人日. *Wenji* 535.

24. Jao's note: Few historical events are recorded for Mengshan 蒙山. Li Deyu's 李德裕 son Ye 燁 was once rusticated to Mengzhou, where he was governor of Lishan 立山. Ye wrote a funerary inscription for his wife, née Zheng, of Xingyang 滎陽: "She passed away in 855 while away from home in Mengzhou. She was temporarily encoffined south of Zijigong in Mengzhou." I do not know where Zijigong was in the Tang. Li Shangyin has an "Untitled Poem" that begins "Through ten thousand leagues of wind and waves …" [*Quan Tang shi* 541.6248]. Interpreters say that this was composed for Ye in Jiangling. While Deyu was exiled to Yaishan 崖山 [modern Xinhui 新會 county, Guangdong] he composed the *Record of Bottomless Sorrow* 窮愁志.

25. Du Fu once applied this expression to himself, but originally Confucius had described himself as a wanderer in all four directions. See *Li ji zhengyi* 6.7a.

Sent to My Elder Yu Ruizheng[26]

Two poems that place Jao's situation as a refugee in time of war in context of classical and literary precedents.

#1

連月失名城	Our great cities are lost each month,
勢如拉枯朽	Disaster arriving fast as deadwood snapping.
反怕消息來	Now I fear that any news should come,
寸心亦何有	For what will survive in my inchlong heart?
六合驚塗炭	I'm startled at the mud and ashes that occupy all Six Directions;[27]
微生同敝帚	Feel my life insignificant as a tattered broomstick.
重華今渺冥	The age of Twin Glory now seems remote,[28]
誰是格苗手	Who will raise a hand to trim these shoots?[29]
蠻貊懷忠信	The Man and Mo here harbor loyalty and devotion,
詩書開戶牖	Through *Odes* and *Documents* I open a window to the outside.[30]
寄聲慮不達	Sending out my voice I fear it does not reach the destination,
城闉屢搔首	Scratching my head over again on the city walls and barricades.
平生歷鋒鏑	Through this life I have encountered spear and arrowpoint,
已成喪家狗	Now I am become no more than a stray dog.[31]
怯除戎馬氣	To eliminate the stench of war-horses,
端恃一杯酒	All it takes is one glass of wine.
放心浩劫前	I take comfort thinking how before this plunder began,
有藤大如斗	There were vines growing lush and big as a bushel.[32]

---

26. 寄懷俞瑞徵丈以尚有秋光照客衣為韻. *Wenji* 541. These are two poems from a set of seven whose rhymes are chosen to match the words in the line "There still remains autumn light, illuminating a traveler's clothes" 尚有秋光照客衣.

27. The six directions are the four cardinal directions, plus the sky above and earth below.

28. "Twin Glory" refers to an enlightened age, such as one that had both a Yao and a Shun.

29. "Trimming the shoots" refers to subduing foreign tribes.

30. The reference to the foreign tribes of Man and Mo suggests the remoteness of the location, but in the next line Jao asserts that he remains connected to civilization through his command of the textual tradition.

31. "Dejected as a stray dog" (literally "a dog that has lost its home") comes from a description of Confucius given by his disciple Zigong when Confucius was standing outside the walls of Zheng. See *Shi ji* 47.1921.

32. It was said that in this area there were vines growing thick enough over the river that men could walk across them.

#2

山居等蟪蛄	Dwelling in the mountains like the late summer cicada,
不復知春秋	I no longer know if this is spring or fall.[33]
死鑽舊紙堆	I steadfastly drill through a pile of old paper,
閉門當遠遊	Closing my door I seem to roam faraway.
不敢學虞卿	I do not dare to emulate Yu Qing,
著書說窮愁	Who wrote a book telling of bottomless sorrow.[34]
願如梁江總	I'd rather be a Jiang Zong as in the Liang dynasty,
還家尚黑頭	Who returned home with hair still black.[35]
故鄉不可望	I cannot even gaze in the direction of my home,
淚與浮雲浮	While my tears drift alongside the drifting clouds.
亦知非吾土	I too know that this is no land of mine:
日日強登樓	Each day I climb unwilling up the tower again.[36]

---

33. Zhuangzi uses this cicada as an example of a creature with an extremely limited conception of the universe's scale, since its lifespan does not even fill an entire year. See *Zhuangzi* 1.11.

34. Yu Qing was a strategist of the Warring States period who wrote a book (*The Springs and Autumns of Yu Qing*) criticizing the policies of the various states (*Shi ji* 76.2375). For the *Record of Bottomless Sorrow*, see the previous poem.

35. Jiang Zong 江總 (519–594) spent a number of years as a refugee in southeastern China, only returning in 563 when he was forty-five years old. Du Fu referred to this fact in his poem "Ditty on Traveling in Old Age" 晚行口號, writing "Far off I am shamed by Jiang Zong of the Liang, / Still black-haired when he returned home." See *Du shi xiangzhu* 5.383.

36. Like Wang Can 王粲 (177–217), who wrote an "Essay on Climbing a Tower" longing for his homeland. That poem is translated in Knechtges, *Wen xuan*, 2:237–242.

The Winter Solstice[37]

This is an effective piece of regulated verse relating the poet's displacement and suffering to the state of the country as a whole. "Rice and millet" is an allusion to poem #65 in the classic Book of Odes, *a lament for the ruins of the ancient Zhou capital.*

心折路迷正愴然	My heart frustrated and my path mistaken, I find myself distraught;
陽生冬至朔風前	Yang energy begins to rise at the solstice, and the North Wind to blow.
一身異縣仍三徙	I am a single body in another land, now thrice removed,
九死辭家又六年	Dying nine times over, away from home six years too long.
破壁曆殘驚歲暮	With the calendar turned over on the ruined wall, I'm startled the year is ending.
碧江山赭失秋妍	Hills of ochre along emerald rivers have lost their autumn charm.
南東行處悲禾黍	Traveling southeast I grieve with the "rice and millet";
觸眼荒疇不復田	For I gaze upon the barren fields I know will not be plowed again.

---

37. 冬至. *Wenji* 544.

Essay on Horse Manure[38]

When Chaozhou had been occupied for one year, famine spread. People were reduced to collecting horse manure and sifting through it for grains of millet to eat. When I heard of this it filled me with grief, and so I composed this poem.[39]

豈大道之在冀兮	Can the Great Way be found in excrement as well?[40]
或齊觀夫糇糧	Or can one regard it equally with millet or fodder?
纇異類之不仁兮	How outrageous that another people should be so unfeeling
驅降民於餓鄉	As to drive the defeated masses into the land of starvation.
5 振草酪既不得兮	Offering grasses or curds would not sate them,
掘鳧茈且未央	Nor could digging up water chestnuts suffice.[41]
仰肥馬之驍騰兮	Look up at the proud leaping of the fatted stallions,
厰充牣乎稻粱	Their mangers overflowing with rice and millet.
可以人而不如馬兮	How is it possible to be a man and still be less than a horse?
10 鼓枵腹而神傷	Though starved bellies are distended, their spirits suffer.
將攘奪而無力兮	They are willing to loot and plunder but lack the strength,
妄意夫皁櫪之秕糠	And daydream of the chaff and husks in the stable—
意秕糠兮不得	When chaff and husks, they know, cannot be found,
嗟裁屬兮弱息	Alas, they gasp and wheeze for shortness of breath.

---

38. 馬矢賦. *Wenji* 280. The poem was apparently written in 1940. The text includes Jao's own notes identifying certain key allusions. "Essay" here and below is a free translation of the genre name *fu*, also translated "rhapsody."

39. Jao's postface (*Wenji* 285): When the War of Resistance began, I fled to the southwest. Each time I climbed to a high place and gazed into the distance, I would take up a brush and express my feelings. Those that have been preserved in a bamboo chest are just these six pieces. My student Jia Fumin of Yiyang, who worked at the Guozhuan, was the one who recorded these. It would be a pity to discard them, so I have kept these works of my youth, and edited them for printing. The "Catalogue of Arts and Letters" in the *History of the Former Han Dynasty* records the names of the writers of rhapsodies (*fu*), even when they only have one or two pieces. Though these insignificant things are no more impressive than a broomstick, I am fond of them anyway. As those who suffer sing of their hardships, thus I express my feelings here, lodging in these poems the miseries of that time, in the hope of finding a reader in some other age. As for their literary value I dare say nothing.

40. The Great Way (i.e., the Dao) is the just rule proclaimed as ideal by early Chinese thinkers. Zhuangzi says that the Way is universal, and can even be found amid feces and urine. See *Zhuangzi* 22.750.

41. The solution employed during a famine under the reign of Wang Mang. See *Hou Han shu* 11.467.

I | TAKING REFUGE

15	惟飢炎之方盛兮	When the flames of hunger are at their peak,
	苟垂涎兮馬矢之餘皂	They salivate at the horse manure left in the stable,
	拾白粲於污腸兮	Gather the ivory kernels from polluted intestines,
	延殘喘於今夕	Extending their wretched gasps through one evening more.
	哀鮮民之無知兮	Alas for the ignorance of the common people!
20	胡蒙恥而戀生	What shame they endure for their attachment to life.
	捐盜哺而喀喀兮	Discarding the stolen food they vomit out,
	獨不見夫瞀瞀之爰精	As if they did not know of the half-blind Yuan Jing.⁴²
	有嗟來而不食兮	Once, because it was offered in pity, a man refused provision—⁴³
	況為味非潔清	But that was not on account of its impure taste.
25	孰使異物遒其相迫兮	What causes these peculiar objects to harry us so keenly?
	悲故國之腥羶	I lament how my own country has been polluted.
	繄馬通之屬饜兮	Alas, that men should eat their fill of horse manure!—
	自書傳而有焉	Though in ancient documents there is talk of such things:
	農稷煮汁以漬穜兮	Farmers boiled it to fertilize the late-ripening seedlings,
30	蒔百谷以食我	They raised the hundred crops to feed the people.⁴⁴
	葛縛銅薦丹砂兮	Ge Hong tied up bronze with it, cooked cinnabar with it,
	又熅之以為火	And heated it to make a fire.⁴⁵
	吳誚元遜可啖矢兮	In Wu they mocked Yuanxun for eating dung,
	恪謂太子宜食卵	And he told the Prince he might as well eat eggs⁴⁶
35	果所出之雷同兮	(Since these are fruits of exactly the same process).
	寧古是而今不可	How is our case today any different from those ancients?
	覽宇宙之修遼兮	Considering the immeasurable breadth of this universe,
	軫人類之幺麼	How wretched and insignificant is the human race!

---

42. Yuan Jingmu 爰精目 (also written 爰旌目) was starving to death on the road, to the point where his vision had become blurred, when a thief who was passing fed him back to health. When Yuan discovered the food had belonged to a thief, he vomited it back up and perished. See *Liezi jishi* 8.263–264.

43. The *Li ji* tells a story of a starving man who refused the food offered by Qian Ao 黔敖 (a nobleman from Qi), because Qian Ao's summons was too rude. The man then starved to death. See *Li ji zhengyi* 10.22a/b.

44. This agricultural practice is discussed by Wang Chong 王充 (27–100?), in *Lunheng jiaoshi* 16.716.

45. Several alchemical formulas involving horse manure are recorded in *Baopuzi nei pian jiaoshi* 16.288–289.

46. The prince of Wu told Zhuge Ke 諸葛恪 (203–253) to eat horse manure. He replied that the prince might as well eat eggs because the two come from the same place. See *San guo zhi* 64.1430.

	萃芳鮑乎一室兮	The fragrant and the putrid share a single chamber,
40	淪康莊於嵬瑣	Craft and trickery are rife along the thoroughfares.
	獨悲心之內激兮	Alone, my grieving heart is ravaged inside me,
	羌誰碎此枷鎖	Who can I find to break these shackles?
	感鹽尸之載車兮	I am saddened by the salted bodies that fill up carts,[47]
	閔滔天之奇禍	Lament this catastrophe that swells up to Heaven.[48]
45	瞻溝壑之悠悠兮	Look upon the vastness of ditches and gutters,
	蔽白骨以蓬蒿	Covering white bones with fleabane and rushes.
	苟餓夫而可敦以義兮	I would inquire of those do-gooders like Qian Ao:
	吾將訊諸黔敖	Even a man on the brink of starvation can preserve his honor.[49]

---

47. The vicious warlord Qin Zongquan 秦宗權 (?–889), one of Huang Chao's 黃巢 confederates, used cartloads of salt-preserved human bodies as provisions for his troops. See *Xin Tang shu* 225B.6465.

48. Words used to describe the catastrophe of a great flood in the *Book of Documents*. See *Shangshu zhengyi* 2.19b.

49. The translation reverses the order of the lines in this final couplet. "Qian Ao" refers back to the story alluded to in ll. 21–24, of the starving man who rejected a gift of food from Qian Ao because it was offered in pity.

Essay on White Clouds[50]

In the winter of 1941, I was still wearing mourning clothes in honor of my grandmother. How miserable it was! Lodging far off in a strange land, exhausted from climbing mountains and crossing rivers to get there; yet after such disaster and bereavement, how trivial seems this pain at merely being a refugee. I cannot find the daylilies of forgetting, let alone give the comfort of "thorn-bushes."[51] Sobbing I have composed this essay, to reach out toward the Yellow Springs of the underworld. When will I ride a vessel of return? I make offerings to my ancestors from a pauper's hut. The text reads:

仰白雲之孤飛兮	I gaze up to the white clouds in their solitary flight,
思王母之劬勞	Think of my queenly grandmother and her efforts for my sake.
扇凱風於寒泉兮	Fanning a "gentle breeze" in the "cold springs,"[52]
極孺慕先二毛	How profound is filial longing, even for this breed of dichromatic hair![53]
昔予之始墜地兮	Long ago when I had just descended to earth,
既延禍於母氏	Catastrophe already came to my own mother.
賴祖慈之畜腹兮	Relying on grandmotherly love since I was in the womb,
固無微而不至	There was nothing so trivial it did not concern her.
恩淪髓而莫報兮	Her marrow-deep love I cannot requite,
顧令伯已愧死	I feel a mortal shame before good Lingbo.[54]
忽出國門而騎瘦馬兮	All at once I leave the gates of my country on a gaunt horse.
豈烏烏之所堪	How is this something that a sigh alone can make bearable?
遭胡塵之決溔兮	The dust trails of the invaders cover a vast expanse,
悲踰垣之曾參	And I lament the "fence-jumping" of Zeng Shen.[55]

---

50. 白雲賦. *Wenji* 282.
51. *Odes* 32, celebrating the filial piety of seven sons toward their mother, begins: "When a gentle wind from the south / Blows to the heart of those thorn-bushes." See Waley, *Book of Songs*, 28.
52. For "gentle breeze" see previous note. The phrase "cold springs" is an allusion to the same poem.
53. "Dichromatic hair" (hair of two colors) refers to the appearance of gray hairs, or the onset of old age. Pan Yue famously complained of this condition when he was only thirty-two.
54. Lingbo is Li Mi 李密 (224–287), who was raised by his grandmother and became renowned for his grandfilial piety toward her.
55. Zeng Shen was a disciple of Confucius and the author of the *Classic of Filial Piety*. Once someone of the same name committed murder. Someone told his mother this, but she replied, "My son would not murder." When told again, she kept on quietly weaving as before. When told a third time, she tossed away the shuttle and fled, climbing over a wall in her flight. The story shows her faith in her son. See *Zhanguo ce jianzheng* 4.252 (Qin II).

違膝下而屑屑兮	I depart the love of my parents' lap, hurried and harried,
攀長條之鬖鬖	Climb up the long branches that grow rough and ragged.
轢予車於峻阪兮	I rolled my carriage up the precarious slopes,
幾迴王陽之羸馭	Rounding the curves on my frail horse, through the Wang Yang pass.[56]
咨孤蒙之惴惴兮	Alas, as an orphaned son, trembling in fear,
望山川而窶步	I gazed at the mountains and rivers that block my step.
下東江之浩渺兮	I sailed off far along the East River,[57]
涕與海而俱注	My tears flowing together with the ocean.
滥吾茬此香爐峰兮	At last I arrived here at Censer Peak,[58]
眷白頭之倚閭	Thinking of the concerns of my white-haired parents.
忽雙鯉其先頒兮	Now that I have already shared the double carp,[59]
猶慮乎朝食而無魚	Still I worry that there will be no fish at breakfast.
感春暉而悕危亂兮	I was grateful for spring sunshine as I regretted this war,
復泗下之交如	My tears poured down again in crisscross lines.
恨日月之逾邁兮	Frustrated that the sun and moon hurried along,
歷三歲於茲土	I endured for three years in this land.
豈懷安之敗名兮	How could you ruin your name through longing for idle repose?[60]
汝而忘夫故宇也	Is it that you have forgotten our old home?"[61]
曰起居猶未遑兮	Alas: "For sleeping and waking we never have the time,
伊玁狁之故也	And it is all on account of the Xianyun."[62]
列丘陵而壅隔兮	The hills and mounds block and obstruct me,
睨故都其遼遠	I see my old hometown in the remote distance.
慨晨昏而罔定省兮	Repining morning and night, with no way to care for my parents,[63]
腸一兮而萬轉	By each sigh my innards are twisted ten thousand times.

---

56. The "Wang Yang route" 王陽道 was a mountain route famed for its difficulty. See *Hou Han shu* 76.3229.

57. The East River is an eastern tributary of the Pearl River, but it is not clear if the geographical terms here describe an actual journey, or simply evoke a sense of displacement.

58. Censer Peak was a famous site on Mount Lu in Jiangxi province.

59. There is a story of a filial daughter who served her mother-in-law and a neighbor two carp each morning. See *Hou Han shu* 84.2783.

60. Like Chong'er 重耳 (Duke Wen 文 of Jin 晉), who was rebuked by his wife for enjoying his idle repose rather than continuing his quest. See *Zuozhuan*, Duke Xi, year 23.

61. These questions are posed by Jao's grandmother.

62. The Xianyun were of the northern enemies of the Chinese, as in *Odes* 167/1. This couplet is a rough quotation from that poem.

63. More specifically, to help them prepare for bed in the evening and ask of their well-being in the morning. See *Li ji zhengyi* 1.18a.

聆金相之殄瘁兮	I know your golden image is troubled and sleepless,
心蹙踳而不安	My heart is wrought with worry and cannot rest.
恩縮地而無術兮	I regret I have no magic art for condensing space,
望驚波之漫漫	While I gaze at endless rows of onrushing waves.

忿欃槍其東出兮	I grieve at the comet that appears in the East,
厲烽煙於瑤島	And beacon fires on the carnelian islands of the immortals.
絕關梁而不通兮	The passes and bridges are severed and cannot be crossed,
欲呼天閽而莫告	I want to knock on Heaven's door but cannot make my appeal.

聘噩耗之遙傳兮	I was startled to hear the evil report transmitted from afar;
忍徒跣而雞斯	I struggle to walk on barefoot with only a hairpin.[64]
乾我肝而焦我肺兮	My liver is parched and my lungs are baked;
獨長號而漣洏	All alone, I wail ceaselessly and weep in torrents.
初疑信其參半兮	At first I am divided halfway between doubt and belief,
猶望望而汲汲	Still full of hope and still desperately longing.
冀魂夢之一通兮	If only our souls could once be joined in dream!
終焉悵惚怳而莫及	But never can my sorrow and my sighs reach her.

哀鳥獸之失群兮	I lament that birds and beasts are separated from their herds,
必反巡其故鄉	And must return to seek out their native places.
尚鳴號而踟躕兮	They still must sob and scream, and linger here,
或踰時而回翔	Though some after a while might soar back.
彼燕雀猶有啁噍之傾兮	Even swallow and sparrow must chirp and cry in sadness,[65]
況生民之貞良	And likewise the loyal and decent among the people.
恐寥廓而無歸兮	I fear to be lost and alone and never to return,
託餘情乎寒螿	To liken my lasting feeling to the cicada announcing winter.
潊哀思於無垠兮	My grieving thoughts extend beyond all bounds;
瞻雲樹而趨蹌	Looking up at the clouds and trees I keep hurrying along.
雖百身而莫贖兮	Though I had one hundred lives I could not save hers;
寧盡乎期年之通喪	Nor could I spend an entire year in total mourning.
披麻衣而踊悲兮	I'll put on hemp garb and fall prostrate in grief:
究年歲而不敢忘	Until my lifespan is done I will never forget her.

---

64. After the death of one's parents one was expected to wear a hairpin and go barefoot. See *Li ji zhengyi* 56.14a.

65. The example of how all living things are touched by emotion comes from *Li ji zhengyi* 58.2a.

II
Western Parallels

Jao spent several years traveling in Europe and America. Though his scholarship was focused on Chinese culture and its broader Asian environment, he was by no means ignorant of the West. In his visits to Europe, in particular, he sought out important literary monuments like the tombs of great poets, and often used these visits as the occasions for verse. In these poems, and most explicitly in the multilingual notes that accompany them, he demonstrates considerable familiarity with literature in English, French, and German. However, his encounters with foreign poets tend to lead him back, ultimately, to reflections on Chinese literature and thought.

In the preface to a collection of ci lyrics from 1979, Jao describes a journey through the Alps and recalls that Rimbaud had preceded him there:[1]

> The French poet Arthur Rimbaud once met a blizzard here as he crossed the Alps on foot. Rimbaud at this time had already abandoned poetry and was setting forth on a long journey in search of the secrets of the Orient. He was feeling dejected, as one can perhaps see already in his poem "Le bateau ivre." That is entirely different from my own sense of freedom and relaxation here. The scenery is not dissimilar, but East and West have different tastes—that's inevitable.

In this case he emphasizes the disjunction between Chinese and European cultures, but more frequently, Jao likes to entertain parallels and resemblances between Chinese culture and the scenes and people he encounters in Europe and America. He draws freely for these comparisons from his own mental treasure house of Chinese texts. These range from an amusing coincidence ("Queens Town") to world-historical reflections ("On the Ruins of the Colosseum in Rome"). Jao generally holds out some hope for the possibility of understanding that spans continents and cultures, as when he praises Donald Holzman's book on Ruan Ji by writing that "if Lord Ruan were aware of it, he would surely be surprised to find an understanding friend a thousand ages apart."[2]

---

1. Preface to "Gu cun ci" 古村詞 (*Wenji* 739).
2. *Wenji* 117.

On the Ruins of the Colosseum in Rome[3]

There is a well-established genre in China of poems reflecting on history and fate at an important site from antiquity. It is a natural extension of the genre to take in a site from abroad, as in these quatrains.

#1

城旦艱難八載成	Slaves building the wall labored eight years to complete it;
劫灰歷歷古今情	Out of these ruins we can perceive the past's distance.
穹廬猶是凌霄漢	This vaulted hall still stands, brushing against the heavens;[4]
六百年間恨不平	Across six centuries, that resentment has not yet been placated.

#2

陵阜茫茫帶日曛	The endless crests of hills are bathed in sunset gleams,
基局固護想雄勳	The walls and battlements form a sturdy defense that recalls heroic deeds.
可憐馬磴成奇戮	How wretched, these massacres achieved on stirrups!
殘霸誰教免豆分	Who can teach the surviving hegemon to avoid a peapod-like partition?[5]

#3

手格千群付一嚬	Fighting by hand a thousand enemies with just a wrinkled brow,
喑嗚林木動星辰	An angry roar through the forest stirs the constellations.
罿罘漫野今安在	Where now are those nets that covered the arena?
角觝寧哀待死人	Do wrestlers still mourn the others condemned to death?

#4

門鎖修齡白日長	Living to old age behind closed doors, the sun stays bright outside;
人間換盡舊伊涼	In this world there's nothing like those old tunes of Yi and Liang.[6]
雄獅猛士真何益	Fierce lions and mighty warriors, what did they truly gain?
未解拽屍意可傷	How lamentable that their corpses were dragged away still unenlightened.[7]

---

3. 羅馬圓劇場 (Colosseo) 廢址. *Wenji* 366.

4. *Qionglu* 穹廬 normally refers to a yurt, but is adapted by Jao to refer to another foreign type of building—perhaps a necessary maneuver when using classical Chinese to describe European cultural settings.

5. A "peapod-like partition" is a common figure for the division of a country, often combined with the image of a sliced melon.

6. Yizhou and Liangzhou were prefectures on the frontier regions of the Han, so their tunes are representative of the music of an age of war and violence.

7. In the Chan classic *Records of Transmission of the Lamp* (*Chuan deng lu* 傳燈錄), "dragging the corpse out" is described as one way of understanding the meaning of Bodhidharma's coming from the West. See *T* 2076:51.267b.

#5

欲譜無愁果有愁	I'd like to write a "melody without melancholy, but melancholy still";
北齊歌吹亦溫柔	The songs and airs of Northern Qi were actually soft and gentle.[8]
白楊風起多冤鬼	In the white poplars a breeze stirs up countless wronged souls;[9]
擲盡頭顱可自由	Only by lopping off skulls could they achieve freedom.

---

8. This couplet refers to Li Shangyin's "Northern Qi Dynasty Song: Melody without Melancholy, But Melancholy Still" 無愁果有愁曲北齊歌 (*Quan Tang shi* 540.6204). The Northern Qi ruled northern China from 550 to 577, which was actually a period of great violence.

9. Li Shangyin wrote of angry spirits amid white poplars in the "Northern Qi Dynasty Song" mentioned above.

On First Entering the Mountains[10]

This poem belongs to a set of poems on the Swiss Alps composed according to the rhymes of Xie Lingyun. It imitates both the dramatic scenery and philosophical conclusion of Xie's own poems, even though the specific images belong to Jao.

漸春山戀人	As spring approaches, the hills grow fonder of men,
延我到蘿屋	And seem to invite me into a house of lichen.
秋毛經冬骨	Autumn hairs in winter are exposed to bone,
飄葉復槁木	The drifting leaves again become withered trunks.
幾曾歷滄桑	How many times have mulberry groves turned to ocean?
誰為剖心曲	Who would dare to carve open his heart for display?
春來山如笑	When spring comes the hills seem to smile upon us,
與我相傾屬	We gaze more closely upon each other.
敢憚千里遙	Why fear a distance of a thousand miles?
呦呦思鳴鹿	You-you, I think of the calling deer.[11]
天長況夢短	The days grow longer but our dreams are brief,
有生悲無樂	For to live is merely sorrow without pleasure.
青山縱不語	Though the turquoise hills do not speak,
亦自感休戚	Still somehow they are moved by my travails.
此情可成丹	Could I brew from these passions some elixir?
我欲問抱朴	I would like to ask the One Who Embraces Simplicity.[12]

---

10. 初入山. *Wenji* 390–391. Based on the rhymes of Xie Lingyun's poem "Passing the White Bank Pavilion" 過白岸亭 (*Xie Lingyun ji jiaozhu* 111).

11. This line quotes the first line of *Odes* 161, a celebration of hospitality.

12. The "One Who Embraces Simplicity" is *Baopuzi*, the title of a treatise on alchemy and philosophy attributed to Ge Hong 葛洪 (284–364).

II | Western Parallels * 39

Ilustration 3. *Lotus and Couplet* (2002).
In this composite work of painting and calligraphy by Jao, the image of the lotus blossoms is framed by a couplet by Xie Lingyun. The couplet says: "Though practical affairs are governed by the Doctrine of Names, / The Way passes above by means of Divine Principles." It is quoted from Xie Lingyun's "Written by Imperial Command When I Accompanied the Emperor on His Journey to Mount Beigu near Jingkou." Cf. Frodsham, *The Murmuring Stream,* 1:171.

Mont-Blanc[13]

Jao quotes Lord Byron and Charles-Julien Lioult de Chênedollé (1769–1833) on the famous mountain, and adapts their lines into his own poem.

瀰沙用構白	A whiteness constructed of pristine sand,
著粉堆冰山	A powder that piles up to make an iceberg:
寒颸崩崖吼	Under freezing gales the plummeting precipices howl,
哄日明危湶	The clamorous sun illumines a precipitous stream.
雕透傷斧刃	The completed sculpture abhors the axe's touch;[14]
吟嘯思前賢	Chanting and whistling we recall the worthies of the past.
坤軸昔曾折	The axle of the Earth was bent here long ago;
天衢若可阡	The thoroughfares of Heaven seem like paths in a field.
硠硠驚走石	Crashing and cracking, the rolling stones surprise;
悄悄飛冷煙	Swiftly and smoothly the cold mists fly past.
今古一成純	Present and past form one pure whole;
誰復較蹄筌	But who again will worry over hare-trap and fish-net?[15]
群山此為君	Of all the mountains this one is sovereign;
雲衣萬壑傳	A garment of clouds over myriad ravines. [16]
象冥定天秩	Phenomena were shadowy before their natural ranks were determined;
理幽分化前	Principles obscure before the transformations were differentiated.

---

13. *Wenji* 390. To the rhymes of Xie Lingyun's "Ru Huazigang shi Mayuan di san gu" 入華子崗是麻源第三谷 (*Xie Lingyun ji jiaozhu* 288).

14. The sculpture abhors more carving because it is already perfect and needs no artificial elaboration.

15. This line alludes to one of the most famous passages in *Zhuangzi* on the relation between language and understanding: "The reason for the net is the fish; when you obtain the fish you forget the net. The reason for the snare is the rabbit; when you obtain the rabbit you forget the snare. The reason for the words is the sense; when you obtain the sense you forget the words. If only I could meet a man who has forgotten words, and share words with him!" See *Zhuangzi* 26.944.

16. This couplet develops Byron's lines: "Mont-Blanc is the monarch of mountains … in a robe of clouds, with a diadem of snow"; and Chênedollé's: "Voilá donc ce Mont-Blanc monarque des montagnes."

只愁月色孤	I only fear that the moon's aspect is too solitary;
猿狖啼潺湲	Gibbons cry and shriek by flowing waters.
艱險駭將壓	"In mountains overwhelming, come and crush me!"—
余悸訝同然	Now that I am here I am equally astonished.[17]

---

17. Cf. Byron again: "Ye toppling crags of Ice! / Ye avalanches, whom a breath draws down / In mountains overwhelming, come and crush me."

Mont-la-ville[18]

In 1966 Jao visited France, where he shared his erudition with French sinologists. Paul Demiéville, the prolific Swiss scholar of Chinese literature and Buddhism, took Jao on a hiking expedition in the Alps. During the trip Jao composed a series of quatrains from which this poem is taken.

一上高丘百不同	Ascend one high hill and everything looks different:
山腰犬吠水聲中	Dogs bay on the mountainside amid the sound of waters,
葡萄葉濕枝頭雨	With grape leaves drenched and rain upon the branches,
苜蓿花開露腳風	Clover blossoms open under windswept dewdrops.

---

18. *Wenji* 402.

Two Poems about Auvergne[19]

These quatrains on the French countryside hint at the landscapes of Jao's imagination superimposed on the visual impressions of his journey.

Lac de Guery

平湖芳草碧毿毿	Fragrant grasses on the level lake a riot of emerald,
戴雪遙峰峻宇紺	Snow-crowned peaks far off soar up into the purple heavens.
布暖條風剛酒醒	In the spring wind's blanketing warmth, I've just sobered up.
中天麗日似江南	The glorious sun in Heaven above is just like in Jiangnan.

Lac Pavin

臨湖徒倚兩三松	Strolling around the lake I pass two or three pines;[20]
微徑思尋麋鹿蹤	On a hidden path I hope to find the traces of the elaphure.[21]
雙槳來時人影亂	When the double oars pass by, my reflection is blurred.
小船搖曳出蘆中	A little boat drifts out from among the reeds.

---

19. *Wenji* 384 and 385. These are selected from a set of thirty-six quatrains.
20. In his poem "Visiting a Daoist Master on Mount Daitian But Not Meeting Him," Li Bai writes of "sorrow attaching to two or three pines." See *Li Taibai quanji* 23.1079.
21. The elaphure is a species of deer unique to China, so there is little chance that this hope will be fulfilled in the Auvergne.

Reading Nietzsche's *Also Sprach Zarathustra*[22]

Jao has an affinity for Nietzsche's combination of philosophical acuity, literary grace, and scholarly eruditon. The notes to Jao's original poems contain quotations from Nietzsche's Also Sprach Zarathustra, some in the original German and some in Chinese translation. For instance, Jao mentions his fondness for the lines "Dem Rauche gleich, / Der stets nach kältern Himmeln sucht" (Like the smoke, that always seeks cold Heaven).[23] These poems set the philosopher's thoughts in a Chinese context that provides new insights.

#1

納納乾坤大	"How vast the space encompassed by Heaven and Earth,"[24]
茫茫今何世	What era is this in the infinity of time?
世果有真宰	The world must have some True Carver[25]
生天復生地	Who created Heaven and then created Earth.
天帝尚畀我	"Supposing a Lord of Heaven existed for us,
我安能自制	How could I bear not to make myself one also?"[26]
狂哉尼采言	How wild are the sayings of Nietzsche!
悲歌欲隕涕	His tragic songs make a man want to weep.
如何變彌巫	However frantically they transform themselves,
幾人竊神器	How many people can steal the capacity of a god?
無復假神力	We will not again borrow a god's power,
悍然比上帝	Or vaunt ourselves alongside a Supreme Lord.
炊煙索寒天	Cooking smoke rises in cold weather;
曠野渺無際	The open plain is vast without end.
何日聽雞鳴	When will we hear again the cockcrow,
泱漭天初霽	And sky's first clearing from limitless dark?

#2

彼岸倘可期	If I could predict when I'd reach the opposite shore,
悠悠即長路	I would set out on the long road thither.
崩厓當我前	Plummeting cliff walls right before me,
懸車那可度	How can I cross those carriage-derailing crags?

---

22. 讀尼采薩天師語錄. *Wenji* 374.
23. From an 1884 poem by Nietzsche, "Abschied" (Valediction). See *Nachgelassene Fragmente 1884–1885*, 329.
24. This line is a direct quotation from Du Fu. See *Du shi xiangzhu* 22.1973.
25. The phrase "True Carver" comes from *Zhuangzi* 2.55.
26. This couplet is equivalent to Nietzsche's line: "*Wenn* es Götter gäbe, wie hielte ich's aus, kein Gott zu sein! *Also* giebt es keine Götter." See "Auf den glückseligen Inseln," *Also Sprach Zarathustra*, 110.

我手方高攀	As my arms climb higher and higher,
我眼須下顧	My eyes cannot resist a glance beneath.
兩途俱可愕	Both paths are equally perilous,
捷徑終窘步	I must lose my step in these shortcuts.
躋險豈不艱	Truly it is difficult to ascend that precipice,
傾墜者無數	And those who plummet downwards are many.
深淵諒可懼	But "it is the deep abyss that is to be feared,
峻嶺非所怖	And not the high peaks that cause us terror."[27]
誰能更於此	Who again in circumstances like these
磨勘得妙悟	Could attain miraculous insight through patient labor?

#3

文明果何謂	What after all is civilization?
安在繁華中	How can it be found amid luxury?
五色令目盲	The five colors make the eyes blind;
五音使耳聾	The five tones make the ears deaf.[28]
混沌終自戕	Hundun ultimately destroyed itself;
椎鑿安所窮	When did the chiseling and drilling finish?[29]
理廢寧蘊真	When the pattern is gone, how can one find the genuine?
玄珠墜幽宮	Black pearls plummet through the palace of dark.
茲辰非曩日	This morning is not as in the days of old,
視天更夢夢	And Heaven looks more ambivalent than ever.[30]

---

27. "Nicht die Höhe: der Abhang ist das Furchtbare!" (Not the height but the declivity is terrifying). See "Von der Menschen-Klugheit," *Also Sprach Zarathustra*, 183.

28. *Laozi*, ch. 12.

29. According to Zhuangzi, Hundun, also described as the formless mass at the beginning of the universe, originally had no orifices; two other gods drilled out his seven orifices, one each day, and on the final day Hundun died. See *Zhuangzi* 7.309.

30. *Odes* 192/4.

井泉暮夜鳴	The wellspring gurgles at nightfall,[31]
此意孰與同	But who can understand its meaning?
焉得薩天師	Where may I find a Master Zarathustra,
為洗陰霾空	To clear away the haze and fog from the blue sky?
看看窗牖間	Look up there in the window now—
杲杲日生東	"Resplendently rises the sun in the East!"[32]

---

31. "Nacht ist es: nun reden lauter alle springenden Brunnen. Und auch meine Seele ist ein springender Brunnen" (It is night: now all the soaring fountains speak louder. And my soul too is a soaring fountain). See "Das Nachtlied," *Also Sprach Zarathustra*, 136.

32. *Odes* 62/3. But compare the final sentence of *Also Sprach Zarathustra*: "Also sprach Zarathustra und verliess seine Höhle, glühend und stark, wie eine Morgensonne, die aus dunklen Bergen kommt." See "Das Zeichen," *Also sprach Zarathustra*, 408.

Reading the Poetry of Rimbaud[33]

Jao's affinity for the poetic genius Arthur Rimbaud (1854–1891) comes through clearly in this unique poem, in part homage, in part a medley of some of Rimbaud's most famous phrases with parallels from late Tang poet Li He. Li He, the "demonic talent," like Rimbaud was a prodigy known for his unconventional, haunting imagery. Li He was particularly renowned for evocations of the spirit world and ancient myths. There are tantalizing demonstrations of how a classical Chinese verse rendering of Rimbaud would read.

舟如蝶迷陽	A boat is like a butterfly seduced by sunlight,[34]
飄飄到何方	Floating off to someplace I know not where.
冷眼看乾坤	With cold glance regarding earth and heaven,
熱淚灑平岡	I sprinkle hot tears over level hills.
沉憂虹貫日	Condemned to despair, a rainbow crosses the sun;[35]
隱愛雪充腸	Love concealed like snow fills the entrails.[36]
至道生無名	The ultimate way is born from the Nameless,[37]
嶄新出悲凉	And creativity gives rise to melancholy.[38]
空中傳恨語	Those words of regret transmitted through the air:[39]
百世不敢忘	In a century I would not be able to forget them.
我邦稱鬼才	In our country we call it a "demonic talent,"
長爪差雁行	His untrimmed nails like wild geese in formation.[40]

---

33. 讀 Rimbaud 詩. *Wenji* 398. To the rhymes of Xie Lingyun's "At the Tomb of the Prince of Luling" 廬陵王墓下 (*Xie Lingyun ji jiaozhu* 193).

34. Jao is adapting the opening line of Rimbaud's "Le bateau ivre": "Un bateau frêle comme un papillon de mai."

35. This line may be inspired by Rimbaud's "J'avais été damné par l'arc-en-ciel," in *Une Saison en Enfer*.

36. This line refers to Rimbaud's "Ophélie": "Ciel ! Amour ! Liberté ! Quel rêve, ô pauvre Folle ! / Tu te fondais à lui comme une neige au feu." Jao compares these lines to Bai Juyi's couplet: "The things I have loved in this life: / I loved fire and also adored the snow." See *Bai Juyi ji* 22.498.

37. See *Laozi*, ch. 1: "The nameless is the origin of Heaven and Earth."

38. See introduction for discussion of the line from Baudelaire quoted here in Jao's original note: "Au fond de l'Inconnu pour trouver du nouveau!"

39. This line quotes a *ci* lyric by Zhu Yizun 朱彝尊 (1629–1709), which he used as the epigraph to a collection of his *ci*. See *Zhu Yizun shici xuanzhu*, 149.

40. Li Shangyin mentions in his biography of Li He that he was "gaunt of frame, with connected eyebrows, and long fingernails." See Frodsham, *Goddesses, Ghosts, and Demons*, xv.

萬星燦暮夜	The myriad stars are sparkling through the night,
千鳳騫奇芳	The thousand phoenixes ascend like rare blossoms.[41]
後不見來者	I cannot see those to come in the future,
勇往意何傷	But boldly advancing will not let my will be thwarted.
睿哲天所忌	The sagely ones are often envied by Heaven:
連播豈相妨	Was that why it hindered him in his flight?
滄海窮曛黑	Over the watchet ocean he explored the twilight dark;
歲月念方將	Through the years that passed his thoughts were of the future.
夭枉無足悲	An untimely death need not be lamented,
輝光詎尋常	When its illuminations were never ordinary.[42]
江河萬古流	Rivers have flowed on since ancient times,
盛藻隨風揚	And splendid figures of poetry have risen with the wind.[43]
尚論他與我	We still discuss his "self" and "other,"[44]
餘蘊待平章	But their meaning awaits new interpretation.

---

41. Jao cites Rimbaud's line, "Million d'oiseaux d'or, ô! future Vigueur?" This quotation is also from "Le bateau ivre."

42. The "illuminations" refer to Rimbaud's collection of prose poems "Les Illuminations."

43. The figures are literally "algae," which represents literary ornamentation in classical Chinese.

44. Rimbaud famously wrote "Je est un autre."

At the Tomb of Rainer Maria Rilke[45]

Jao cites Rilke's own epitaph for himself: "Rose, oh reiner Widerspruch, Lust Niemandes Schlaf zu sein unter soviel Lidern!" (Rose, O pure contradiction, the desire to be nobody's sleep under so many lids!)

人間從此變淒寥	The human realm from this position seems a sphere of desolation;
花下高眠意自遙	An inspired nap under the flowers gives the mind some distance.
留有暗香誰省得	Who can understand the faint fragrance left behind?
西風新塚樹蕭蕭	Only the West Wind that rustles the trees over a fresh tomb.

---

45. R.M. Rilke 墓. *Wenji* 403.

Visiting Victor Hugo's Former Residence in the Jardin des Feuillantines[46]

Inspired by thoughts of Victor Hugo, Jao extemporizes on the topic of nostalgia.

古來京洛地	Since ancient times at the Luo capital,
素衣易變淄	White clothes have changed easily to black.[47]
獨有江海人	Alone the traveler across rivers and oceans
高唱秋懷詩	Chants a noble poem of "autumn longings."
落日愛黃昏	At sunset you fall in love with twilight,
玉碎悲素絲	Once jade is shattered you mourn for white silk.
割霜月如鐮	Carving through frost, the moon is like a scythe,
南畝更念茲	In the southern garden I think more keenly of this man.
山鬼一何哀	How sorrowful is that mountain spirit,
歌斷寒颸颸	Her song interrupted by the sough of the icy gale.
聲酸歐陽賦	Ouyang Xiu's rhapsody has a sour tone;
神泣鮑家辭	Bao Zhao's elegy is that of a god in tears.[48]
異曲各示工	In those different melodies each reveals his craft,
蕭條不同時	The sense of desolation that belongs to different ages.
我來戶庭闐	When I arrive, gate and garden are shut up,
躑躅欲安之	And though I dither here, where will I go?
風徽感氣類	In the slight breeze I sense a commonality of forces;[49]
敢效青冥期	How dare I know of the destiny intended by dark spirits?

---

46. Jardin des Feuillantines 訪 Victor Hugo 故居. *Wenji* 396. Composed to match the rhymes of Xie Lingyun's "On First Departing from Shishou City" 初發石首城.

47. As in Lu Ji's 陸機 (261–303) poem "For His Wife on Behalf of Gu Yanxian" 為顧彥先贈婦, where the dust and storms of the capital are said to turn white clothes black. See *Wen xuan* 24.1149.

48. Two famous *fu* writers of the past. Here probably referring specifically to Ouyang Xiu's "Rhapsody on the Sound of Autumn" and Bao Zhao "Rhapsody on the Ruined City," both particularly melancholy pieces.

49. From the text of the first hexagram, Qian 乾, in the *Book of Changes*: "Like voices respond to one another, like forces (*qi*) seek one another out." Cf. Wilhelm-Baynes, 382.

喪明傷西河	Losing his vision he grieved [like Zixia] at West River,[50]
指天比南嶷	Pointing to Heaven [like Qu Yuan] at the Southern Doubter.[51]
清芬不可接	That ethereal fragrance cannot be seized onto,
懷賢增淒其	Recalling those past heroes only increases my melancholy.
但看林木秀	Though I see the trees here in bloom,
颯颯朔風欺	Soughing and sighing the North Wind torments them.[52]

---

50. Confucius' disciple Zixia 子夏, having lost both his son and his eyesight, spent his last years at West River in the ancient kingdom of Wei 魏. See *Li ji zhengyi* 7.8b.

51. Qu Yuan, who was also said to have written the somewhat Job-like "Questions for Heaven," visits this mountain in the poem "Far Roaming." See *Chuci buzhu* 5.172.

52. From "Mountain Spirit" 山鬼 in the "Nine Songs": "The wind soughs and sighs, the trees whistle and whine, / I long for the young lord, and only meet with sorrow." See *Chuci buzhu* 2.81 (and cf. "How sorrowful is that mountain spirit" above).

Recalling Lake Léman[53]

In 1956 I visited the lake on my way to Geneva. Now I find that ten years have passed since that time.

淥水入我夢	Crystalline waters entered into my dream,
所思不可論	But what I am yearning for I cannot tell.
永夜無回波	In the long night there are no returning waves,
斷岸有驚奔	The banks rise precipitously as if startled into flight.[54]
層嶺隱蒼榛	The layered ridges are concealed by gray-green hazel,
幽路襲芳蓀	Dark paths are swept by fragrant iris.
千峰冰雪際	Somewhere between ice and snow the thousand peaks
猶作睥睨屯	Huddle together with glowering stare.
撩人惟春夏	People are made restless by the spring and summer,
警我兼晨昏	Something cautions me at dawn and dusk.
寂默沈萬頃	Ten thousand miles are submerged in silence,
旖旎敞千門	One thousand gates open in elegant array.
平蕪天盡頭	Continuing level all the way to the edge of Heaven,
低樹影空存	The shadows of low trees lurk in the air.
煙外溪娘語	Beyond the mist you hear the voice of a maiden in the streams;[55]
波面姹女魂	The surface of the waves reflects the soul of some beauty.
祁寒至此盡	The Arctic chill extends no further past this point,
湛碧欲流溫	Where sparkling emerald waters prepare to gush out warmth.
殊鄉等吾土	This foreign land is just like my own,
且共樂安敦	Let us delight together in tranquility and truth.

---

53. 憶 Léman 湖. *Wenji* 397. To the rhymes of Xie Lingyun's "Entering Pengli Lake" 入彭蠡湖口 (*Xie Lingyun ji jiaozhu* 281). Lake Léman is more commonly known in English as Lake Geneva. Jao cites lines from Lamartine's poem "Le Lac": "Ainsi, toujours poussés vers de mouveaux rivages, / Dans la nuit éternelle emportés sans retour," and also Shelley's "Clear, Placid Leman … which warms me with Its stillness, to forsake Earth's troubled waters for a surer spring."

54. Cf. Su Shi's "Gazing at Mountains from the River" 江上看山 (*Su Shi shiji* 1.16).

55. Cf. Wu Wenying's line "In sorrow I see the maiden of Yue streams," referring to his concubine in Suzhou (*Mengchuang ci quanji jianshi* 4.298).

Queens Town[56]

This playful quatrain composed in Queenstown, New Zealand, is inspired by a note in Su Shi's Dongpo zhilin 東坡志林 *on his place of exile, Huangzhou: "Yong'an city, fifteen miles east of Huangzhou, is popularly known as Nüwangcheng." Nüwangcheng literally means "Queen's Town." Jao refers to Su Shi by his assumed name "East Slope."*

華燈璀璨盡風情	The lamps glitter like precious stones, full of mood and passion;
不負崎嶇萬里行	It's worth the ten-thousand-mile journey here, however rough.
欲起東坡同遊賞	I'd like to call old East Slope to join me in a visit;
南溟亦有女王城	The Southern Hemisphere has a Queens Town of its own!

---

56. 女皇鎮. *Wenji* 686.

On the Grand Canyon[57]

For Jao the awesome scale of the Grand Canyon seems to dwarf even the mythical mountain of Kunlun. The forces of nature here place in perspective even the great luminaries of human civilization.

赤峰連霄一片紅	Crimson peaks are joined with the heavens in a single sheet of red:
巨靈手自開鴻濛	Some mighty spirit must have carved this out of formless matter.
俯臨無地崑崙小	When I peer down the ground vanishes and Mount Kunlun looks small:
七聖自應迷去蹤	The Seven Sages themselves would lose sight of their footsteps here.[58]

---

57. 大峽谷. *Wenji* 722.
58. Jao's note: There are place names within the canyon in honor of Confucius, Mencius, Vishnu, and other ancient sages.

II | Western Parallels * 55

Illustration 4. *Grand Canyon* (1980s).

Cheung Chau Collection #44[59]

In one of a series of poems matching the rhymes of third-century poet Ruan Ji, Jao correlates traditional Chinese and Western poetics. He draws on the Chinese parallel between the poet and the shaman who passes freely between the spiritual and terrestrial realms, then relates it to Plato's analogy (in the dialogue Ion*) between poetry's efficaciousness and the power of a lodestone (magnet). In a note, Jao adds yet another erudite reference: according to Aristotle's* De anima, *pre-Socratic philosopher Thales also believed that magnets are souls.*[60]

詩成須有神	Spirit is necessary to complete a poem,
神乖理無方	But when spirit is disobeyed the pattern goes astray.
楚人詠靈修	A man of Chu sang of Numinous Perfection,[61]
芳菲襲滿堂	And of sweet odors that filled the whole court.
天機日月行	The mechanisms of Heaven direct the sun and moon,
雕斫徒自傷	While carving and chipping words I grieve in vain.
要如磁石靈	I would prefer to be like the divine lodestone
吸引動三光	That draws and directs the Three Luminosities.[62]
三復伊安篇	Thrice repeating the paragraphs of the *Ion*,
聊此道其常	I'll try to say something of the immutable things.

---

59. *Wenji* 473.
60. See *De anima*, Book I, 405a.
61. The man of Chu is Qu Yuan, who sang of himself in the "Lisao" under the name of Lingxiu, "Numinous Perfection."
62. The Three Luminosities are the sun, moon, and stars.

III

Eastern Visions

Jao has a lifelong interest in the cultures and languages of South and Southeast Asia, reflected in both his scholarship and poetry. The focal point of his interest is Buddhism, which Jao has recognized as one of the main spiritual inspirations for Chinese culture. Thus for the title of his collection of poems on his journeys to Southeast Asia, Jao chose "Collection from the Country of the Buddha" (Foguo ji 佛國集). Most of the poems translated in this section come from the collection, though some are also from later journeys around Asia, including to the western regions of China and central Asia. There are also a couple of memorable poems from Jao's visits to Japan.

In the preface to "Collection from the Country of the Buddha," Jao explains its origins as follows: "In the autumn of 1963, I was studying in India, and on the way back visited Sri Lanka, Myanmar, Cambodia, and Thailand for two full months. Those sites and landscapes were mostly ones that Faxian, Xuanzang, and Yijing did not pass through,[1] and they filled me with emotion and infused me with new ambition. Wherever I visited I would compose some new verses, most of which matched the rhymes of East Slope's ancient-style heptasyllabic poems."[2]

---

1. Faxian 法顯 (337–422), Xuanzang 玄奘 (602–664), and Yijing 義淨 (635–713) are the three famous Chinese monks who traveled west to India during the medieval period.
2. *Wenji* 349.

On the Night-Blooming Kaḍupul[3]

This is Jao's earliest extant poem, composed when he was fifteen years old. The topic is the night-blooming cactus Epiphyllum oxypetalum *(Chinese* youtan hua*). The variety from Sri Lanka that Jao's family had acquired might be known by its Sinhalese name Kaḍupul. This philosophical lyric was an auspicious start to Jao's lifelong engagement with the Indian subcontinent.*

異域有奇卉	From foreign lands there came a splendid bloom,
植茲園池旁	Now planted by the pond in our garden.
夜來孤月明	When night comes and the lonely moon is full,
吐蕊白如霜	You open up your petals white as frost.
香氣生寒水	Fragrant odors appear in the coldest waters,
素影含虛光	Plain reflections contain a hollow gleam.
如何一夕凋	How can you wither in just one evening?
殂謝亦可傷	Yet this death is still to be lamented.
豈伊冰玉質	Can it be that your essence pure as ice and jade
無意狎群芳	Has no desire to dally with the other blossoms?
逐爾離塵垢	I would follow you beyond the dust and filth,
冥然返太蒼	And return through void up into the empyrean.
太蒼安可窮	Into the empyrean—but how can I reach so far?
天道邈無極	The way of Heaven is vast and has no limit.
衰榮理則常	The principle of bloom and blight is constant,
幻化終難測	These illusory changes ultimately hard to fathom.
千載未足修	One millennium is not necessarily a long time,
轉瞬詎為逼	Nor does every instant pass rapidly.
達人解其會	The wise man recognizes the critical moment;[4]
保此恆安息	Preserving this, he remains ever calm and at ease.
濁醪且自陶	Drinking the unfiltered lees and enjoying myself,
聊以永茲夕	I wish I could make this evening last a little longer.

---

3. 優曇花詩. *Qing hui ji* 179. Jao's preface: The Youtan flower originates in Sri Lanka. My family had two of them, which blossomed on moonlit nights, but then withered by morning. We all grieved for them. I wrote this poem to elaborate on this principle that splendid things cannot last.

4. Cf. Hightower, *The Poetry of T'ao Ch'ien*, 125.

Recalling Xuanzang at Kanchipuram[5]

On his own visit to India, Jao recalls the visit of the most famous Chinese visitor to India of history, Xuanzang (602–664), who brought back the Tripitaka of Indian sutras to China, a journey fictionalized in the classic novel Journey to the West. *Kanchipuram is located near the southern tip of the Indian subcontinent in the modern state of Tamil Nadu. At the time of Xuanzang's visit it was the capital of the Pallava dynasty.*

達摩當年附舶處	Here where Bodhidharma once moored his ship,
蒼蒼叢芮塞行路	Lush grasses in fresh clusters cover up the road.
事去何人憶往賢	Now that they are gone, who remembers those past sages?
剩有微風吹蘭杜	Only gentle breezes still blow upon the orchids and pollia.
經過不辨路與橋	Passing there you cannot recognize the roads and bridges,
西風門巷雨瀟瀟	The West Wind sweeping raindrops over gates and alleys.
縱然寶塔凌雲起	Even though the precious stupa rises up piercing the clouds,
丹霞已取木佛燒	Danxia has already taken the wooden Buddha to be burned.[6]
慈恩陳蹟何所有	Where are the traces of the Temple of Generous Blessing today?[7]
牛車困頓臥病叟	Just an oxcart stuck in place, an old man sick in bed.
空思彈舌受降龍	In vain I think of him wielding his tongue to pacify the dragons:[8]
更無梵住供屛守	But no longer are there abodes of piety to worship and honor.[9]
誰殉猛鷙舍中身	Who would sacrifice his flesh to vultures or discard his life midway?[10]
始嘆今人遜古人	For once I must lament how inferior we today are to the ancients.
漸看圓月露松隙	Gradually I perceive the round moon in the gap between the pines,
想見清光猶為君	And seem to see you there still, suffused in pure light.[11]

---

5. 建志補羅懷玄奘法師. *Wenji* 353–354. Following the rhymes of Su Shi's "Yu ju guan" 玉局觀.
6. Danxia was a Chan master said to have burned a wooden statue of the Buddha. See the *Records of Transmission of the Lamp* (*Chuan deng lu* 傳燈錄), *T* 2076: 51.313c.
7. The Ci'en temple was where Xuanzang translated Buddhist sutras at Chang'an.
8. Jao notes that he is borrowing a phrase from Tang poet Li Dongdao 李洞道 here. It was said that Xuanzang taught the *Heart Sutra* to dragons during his journey.
9. Jao notes that the area has been overtaken by the Hindu religion, and that there is only one statue of the Buddha left in all the temples.
10. These two figures of speech are borrowed from a line in Wang Jin's 王巾 (d. 505) "Dhūta Temple Stele Inscription" (*Wen xuan* 59.2535), arguing that a Buddhist believer ought to be willing to sacrifice his own life.
11. These final lines borrow from a poem by Chang Jian 常建. See *Quan Tang shi* 144.1454.

On the Inscriptions by Scribes at the End of Each Scroll from Dunhuang[12]

As an outstanding scholar of Chinese epigraphy, Jao feels a special identification with the scribes whose work was so well preserved in the Dunhuang caves.

#1

墨跡依稀字似蠅	Inky traces are sparse but the characters are like flies,[13]
蜀江魚子剡溪藤	On roe-dyed cloth from Shujiang, on the vines of Shan Creek.[14]
何期折柱揚灰日	How can you expect, after the ashes have been scattered and the pillars broken,[15]
更見奇書出羽陵	To see that marvelous writing appear once more in Yuling?[16]

#2

寫經無酒筆頭乾	Copying sutras without wine, the brush tip goes dry:
萬軸摩挲廢寢餐	Laboring over ten thousand scrolls, no time for sleep or food.
不及晁陳徐討論	Too late to discuss this together with Chao or Chen;[17]
古悲根觸涕汍瀾	Provoked by an ancient sadness I feel my tears pour out.

---

12. 敦煌卷尾每有寫經生題記. *Wenji* 519.
13. A style of calligraphy is called "fly's head" because the characters are so small.
14. Shan Creek vines could be used for papermaking.
15. Yu Xin 庾信 (513–581) described the destruction of the Liang capital: "scrolls on jade rollers to be scattered in ashes, / And Dragon-Pattern swords to hack the pillars." See Graham, *The Lament for the South*, 93.
16. Yuling or Yulin 羽林 was a place said to preserve ancient writings in the mythical biography of Emperor Mu. See *Mu Tianzi zhuan* 5.4a.
17. Chao Gongwu 晁公武 (1105–1180) and Chen Zhensun 陳振孫 (ca. 1183–ca. 1262), two Southern Song bibliographers, never had the chance to consult Dunhuang texts. The caves were sealed in the Northern Song dynasty and only discovered in the early twentieth century.

On Lake Toba[18]

J.G. Frazer in Volume III of *The Golden Bough* once recorded the custom of summoning the soul of a deceased person in this region, on the island of Sumatra in Indonesia. The text he quotes is very like the "Summons to the Soul" in the *Chuci*: "Come back, O soul, whether thou art lingering in the wood, or on the hills, or in the dale."[19] Mount Toba is located to the east of Aceh, whose people are fierce and warlike. There is a bronze bell here that was cast in 1471 during the Ming dynasty.

寧無宋玉解招魂	Is it because Song Yu mastered the summoning of souls
穹谷深林鬼火屯	That spirit fires linger in these winding valleys and occluded groves?
象陣兵銷千載後	One thousand years later the elephant armies are gone,
殘鐘依舊挂黃昏	But the fading echo of this bell hangs as ever in the twilight.

---

18. Toba 湖絕句. *Wenji* 514. This is one of a series of quatrains.
19. Frazer, *The Golden Bough*, 3d Ed., Vol. III, *Taboo and the Perils of the Soul*, 45–46.

Taj Mahal[20]

The Taj Mahal was built as a mausoleum for the third wife of the Mughal emperor, Shah Jahan. There is a tradition of Chinese poetry mourning imperial concubines, or in particular the concubines whom Cao Cao had buried alive in his tomb.

雄心賸欲寄溫柔	The boundless desires of ambitious men alight on gentle targets;
傾國生來有底愁	A kingdom-overturning beauty leaves behind longlasting sorrow.
竟逐名花憔悴損	Striving after famous blossoms men exhaust and destroy themselves;
玉鉤殘夢冷于秋	The jade hook of the moon, a patch of dream, is colder than autumn.
名陵風月異朝昏	The romance of this famous tomb is different at dawn and dusk;
眉嫵遙山帶淚痕	The shimmering beauty of the far-off mountains bears a trace of tears.
莫道霸圖今已矣	Don't speak of those designs of the conqueror that are futile now;
御街墜葉為招魂	The leaves fallen on royal avenues will serve to summon back souls.[21]

---

20. 泰姬陵. *Wenji* 357.
21. "Summoning the Soul" is an ancient custom in China described in the famous poem of this name from the *Chuci* anthology, which was also mentioned in the previous poem.

Visiting Angkor Wat at Night[22]

In a note Jao mentions that another poet, Zheng Huaide 鄭懷德, had written about Angkor Wat already in 1786.

曲徑江通欸乃村	A crooked path and straight river lead to the fishing village;
衝寒何事叩重門	Who braves the cold to knock on these doubled doors?
疑雲成陣蛙爭鼓	It seems the clouds are in formation, frogs croaking like drums.
殘月無聲犬吠昏	The crescent moon is silent, and dogs bark in the twilight.
荇藻陂池悲寂寞	The amaranth and algae of hillside ponds are grieving in the stillness;
龍蛇山澤想軍屯	Dragons and snakes in mountain pools recall fortifications here.
塔鈴不語今何世	The chime in the tower does not tell us what age we belong to now:
聊欲尋詩石尙溫	But I could perhaps find a poem here where the stones are still warm.

---

22. 夜訪吳哥窟. *Wenji* 360. First of two poems.

Illustration 5. *Angkor Wat* (1982).

To the Tune of "Courtyard Full of Fragrances": Recollections at Angkor Wat[23]

In Jao's vision Angkor Wat is haunted by the lingering ghosts of ancient passions.

磵裏縈沙	Covered by sand in the ravine,
溪邊聚葉	gathering leaves by the stream,
古洞時變陰晴	the ancient cavern clears now and then darkens.
蕭條林際	In the silence of the forest
廢殿枕寒英	palace ruins are blanketed by chill blossoms.
湖水平分曠渚	The lake waters divided evenly by a broad islet,
朱欄外	beyond a vermilion railing
綠共波平	the greenery is level with the waves:
人家遠	Households are far off,
空山切響	brief echoes in empty hills
漸急瀉銀箏	where silver flutes gradually quicken.

* * *

芳情	A sense of flowering things:
鷗戲岸	Gulls playing on the shore,
馬嘶峻路	horses neighing on steep paths,
花泛蘭纓	blossoms scattered on orchid-scented capstrings.
漸雲滋岫複	Gradually clouds fill up the cavernous shelves,
樹老滄瀛	trees grow old in azure seas.
坐覺愁生白露	I feel a sadness stirring in the white dew,
更飢鼠	while starving mice
啼夜堪驚	wake me with their chattering in the night.
野風急	The gale is fierce,
芸黃腓草	rue brown and withered grasses:
瘦日下荒城	an emaciated sun descends on the abandoned city.

---

23. 滿庭芳・吳哥窟憶舊. *Wenji* 588. Matching the rhymes of Qin Guan 秦觀 (1049–1100).

To the Tune of "Path through Terraces and Cities": When I Imagine the Palaces of Immortals …[24]

When I imagine the palaces of immortals on divine mountains, I recall my visit long ago to Simhala (Sri Lanka). I roamed through the holy city of Anuradhapura, originally built by Ashoka (304–232 BCE), emperor of the Maurya dynasty. There amid ruined towers and naked bricks, fallen lotus trees and decayed willows, the grasses of meditation are not yet weeded out, and the lamps of wisdom remain bright. These allow our spirits to fly, passing outside the borders of life and death. Now composing this song in accord with the rhymes of Jiang Kui, my heart leaps toward those orchid-scented traces, the sounds of those cloud-like looms and moonlike shuttles—may this too be one way for the children of this age to find enlightenment.

沈郎早作歸魂賦	Master Shen long ago composed the "Rhapsody of the Returning Soul."[25]
荒村不聞人語	In the deserted village you hear no one speak.
怯柳彌天	Timid willows have filled up the sky,
愁荷委地	melancholy lotus blossoms all over the ground,
曾是梵宮深處	this place once rich in Buddhist palaces.
寒蛩莫訴	Don't complain about the sad chirping of the crickets:
正洞府高秋	At the height of autumn in Cavern Treasurehouse,
自鳴仙杼	divine shuttles sing of their own accord.[26]
似到青穹	It seems we have reached the azure heavens,
夷猶鎮日甚情緒	I linger here all day long with a nostalgic feeling.

* * *

靈風吹盡夢雨	A spirit wind blows away the rain of dreams.[27]
又疏鐘斷續	Then far-off bells chime, on and off,
添幾殘杵	adding the sound of pestles half-heard.

---

24. 臺城路：偶作仙山樓閣，憶往歲遊師子國，流連聖城，阿育王始所締構者也。殘塔荒甃，敗荷頹柳，禪草未劃，慧燈猶續，令人神飛生死之表。今茲奮管和姜，馳心蘭迹，雲機月杼，倘亦世間兒女頓悟之資耳。*Wenji* 283.

25. Master Shen is Shen Jiong 沈炯 (503–561), and his *fu* may be found in *Yiwen leiju* 79.1358.

26. Jao compares the scenery here to the home of the immortals (Cavern Treasurehouse), where the shuttles of their looms make a music of their own.

27. Jao adapts a couplet from Li Shangyin's poem "Revisiting the Altar to the Goddess" (cf. Liu, *The Poetry of Li Shang-yin*, 95). The spirit wind is the spring wind.

雨去何方	Where has the rain gone,
風來甚色	and what color is the wind?
樓閣開門無數	Countless towers and halls open up their gates.
雲根獨與	I am accompanied only by cloud wisps.
便玉樹琅玕	Even though jade trees and jasper ornaments remain
漫傷無女	I grieve that my Lady is gone.[28]
冰盤露泣	Dewdrop tears on an icy platter,
水澄圓月苦	in limpid waters the round moon seems suffering itself.[29]

---

28. From the classic poem "Li sao": "I lament there is no Lady on the high hill." See *Chuci buzhu* 1.30.

29. The last four lines use various images from the Chan classic *Wansong laoren pingchang tiantong Jue heshang songgu Congrongan lu* 萬松老人評唱天童覺和尚頌古從容庵錄. See *T* 2004: 48.266a.

Written to Express My Sorrow at Seeing Men Beg for Food As in Ancient Times at the Mouth of the River Ganges[30]

人情儘說了生死	People like to claim that they have transcended life and death,
乞食何因叩鬼門	But then why are these beggars here knocking on the gate of demons?[31]
菜色兩行連彼岸	Two lines of vegetable-starved faces fill the other shore;
情根難斷況愁根	Inseverable is the root of passion—still less so that of melancholy!

---

30. 恒河口乞食如昔，書以志慨. *Wenji* 357.
31. Jao quotes Fang Yizhi 方以智 (1611–1671): "I carry a broken bamboo basket and knock on the gate of demons, offering my wares for sale."

Sequel to the Ballad of the Beauty[32]

A woman in the countryside of northern Burma, loveliness bathed in rich incense, had a comb hairpin with flowers in it, just like the Han custom, so I composed this sequel to the "Ballad of the Beauty," following the original rhymes used by Su Shi.[33]

情深有水難比長	There are passions deep as rivers, but how to compare them?
風吹野花滿頭香	Breezes over the wildflowers, hair full of fragrance,
美人相望不相識	The beauty looks at me without recognition;
秋波脈脈枉斷腸	Her eyes flow like autumn waves touching my heart.
眾花儘是可憐意	The myriad flowers all have their own lovable aspects;
鬱蒸日午奈思睡	In this scorching noonday sun I start to feel drowsy.
忽見陌頭柳色新	Suddenly I see on the edge of the field-path the willows in new guise,
愁牽野草隨風靡	And sorrow drags the wild grasses off with the wind.
深秋南國不知寒	So deep into autumn the southern countries do not yet know cold,
且從茅店歇征鞍	But in their thatched huts relieve the saddles of the journey.
人間未乏周昉筆	This world does not lack the brush of a Zhou Fang,
暫作欠伸背面看	In the moment she yawns I see her figure from behind.[34]
始信東坡言無底	Now I realize that East Slope's words had no basis,
誤把西湖擬西子	When he mistook a West Lake maiden for Miss Xi.[35]
君看草樹連雲齊	Look now how grasses and trees grow level with the clouds,
中有嬌鶯恰恰啼	And among them orioles chirp beguilingly *kyap-kyap*.

---

32. 續麗人行. *Wenji* 359.
33. For the original "Ballad of the Beauty" by Su Shi, see *Su Shi shiji* 16.811.
34. Zhou Fang was a painter of the Tang dynasty, celebrated for his portraits of beautiful ladies. In Su Shi's preface to the original poem, he writes: "Li Zhongmou's house has a painting by Zhou Fang of his own wife, portrayed from behind while yawning, which is exquisite. I wrote this poem about it in jest."
35. The famous beauty Xi Shi, to whom Su Shi also refers in the original poem.

To the Tune of "Hundred-Word Air"[36]

The ancient country of Pagan (in modern Myanmar) chopped down all its forests in order to build its five thousand stupas, and so to this day it remains scorchingly hot. King Narathihapate once carved an inscription here: "To attain Nirvana, just eat three hundred plates of curry every day." His minister Yazathinkya stopped at an oceanfront tower and lamented that our lives are as transient as water plants.

塵沙浩劫	A kalpa of years countless as grains of sand,
矗五千窣堵	five thousand stupas towering above:
隙駒如溜	just time passing swiftly as a pony passing a crevice.[37]
秋草嘗尋人去後	Once amid the autumn grasses I looked for you, afterwards.
猶似火雲燒候	It is still as if fiery clouds have scorched all here,
百殿都蕪	The hundred palaces overgrown with weeds,
萬林斫盡	the myriad forests razed to earth,
濯濯牛山柳	denuded all the willows of Ox Hill:[38]
瓣香一炷	One stick of melon-section incense,
黃衣膜拜今又	yellow-robed monks clasping hands in prayer even today.

                *   *   *

誰向殘甓摩挲	Who will polish these crumbled bricks,
氣吞牛斗	still grandiose enough to swallow the Ox and Dipper?[39]
石上空夸口	You boast in vain upon these rocks.
落日荒荒分曠野	The setting sun's rays spread across the desolate plain,
忽下東南離獸	and the lonely beasts come downhill from the southeast.
飄蕩浮生	This floating life without fixed abode
何如水艸	is not unlike weeds skimming the pond.

---

36. 百字令. *Wenji* 648. Jao's preface: "Reading a guide to Pagan in Myanmar, I immediately recalled visiting the tower of Mingalazedi long ago, and strolling about below it. I used the rhymes of Zhu Yizun's poem on Juyong Pass."

37. "Instantaneous as a pony passing a crevice" is a figure for the brevity of human life originating in *Zhuangzi* 22.746.

38. Mencius discussed how after the trees on Ox Hill were chopped down, you could not even tell how fine they had been. See *Mengzi zhushu* 11B.1a.

39. Two constellations, the Oxherd and the Northern Dipper.

語痛津旁堠	His words were pain-stricken at the watchtower by the dike.[40]
涅槃信否	Whether or not you believe in Nirvana,
白雲還逐蒼狗	white clouds continue chasing after grizzled dogs.[41]

---

40. This line adapts a *ci* lyric on the willow tree by Zhou Bangyan, to the tune of "Prince of Lanling" (see *Qingzhen ji jiaozhu* 31), but also refers back to the local story mentioned in the preface.

41. This is an allusion to Du Fu's "Lamentable" 可嘆: "The floating clouds in the sky look now like white robes, / Then in a moment transform into grizzled dogs." See *Du shi xiangzhu* 21.1830.

To the Tune of "Charms of Niannu": On Mount Fuzhou[42]

A picturesque poem on Tangkuban Parahu (in Chinese Fuzhou, "Inverted Boat"), one of the tallest volcanoes in Indonesia.

危欄百轉	Turning one hundred times at the high railing,
對蒼崖萬丈	facing the blue-green cliffs that rise ten thousand feet,
風滿羅袖	breezes fill my gauze sleeves.
試撫當年盤古頂	I'd like to touch the ancient peak of Pangu,
眞見燭龍虛阜	and meet face to face the Lamp Dragon on this hollow hillock.
薄海滄桑	Mulberry groves turn into oceans,
漫山煙雨	whole mountains are covered in mist and rain,
折戟沉沙久	Broken halberds are buried for ages in the sand[43]
巖漿噴處	where the lava streams out.
巨靈時作獅吼	Some vast spirit roars like a lion here.

                *   *   *

只見古木蕭條	Now I only see the ancient trees bare,
斷杈橫地	Riven branches across the ground
遮遏行人走	block this traveler's way.
蒼狗寒雲多幻化	Grizzled dogs and winter clouds exhibit endless transformations[44]
長共夕陽廝守	ever accompanying the sun as it sets.
野霧蒼茫	The fog on the plain forms a vortex of gray,
陣鴉亂舞	formations of crows dancing in confusion.
衣薄還須酒	My robes are thin and I thirst for wine,
世間猶熱	This realm is still scorched
火雲燒出高岫	by gusts of fire out of the high crags.

---

    42. 念奴嬌・覆舟山. *Wenji* 647. *Ershi shiji shi da jia ci xuan* 302–303.
    43. From Du Mu's 杜牧 (803–852) "Red Cliff." Cf. Owen, *The Late Tang*, 292.
    44. As in the final line of the previous poem, the clouds transforming into dogs are Du Fu's figure for mutability.

Inscribed on the Wall at Mogao Grotto[45]

This poem shows Jao's appreciation for the scribes of Dunhuang, whose work was miraculously preserved at Mogao and other sealed caves for a millennium.

河湟入夢若懸旌	The Yellow and Huang Rivers enter my dreams like banners trailing;[46]
鐵馬堅冰紙上鳴	Iron horses and solid ice call out from these manuscripts.
石窟春風香柳綠	Stone grottoes in the spring breeze, green of the wild olive:
他生願作寫經生	In my next life I would rather be a scribe and copy sutras.

---

45. 莫高窟題壁. *Wenji* 673. Jao's note: I composed this while visiting Mogao Grotto in September 1981. I recall a Tang poet wrote these verses: "Snowy crags pierce the blue void, / Cloud towers built upon emerald space. / Layered passes in thousands transmit the sunlight, / Each opening sideways to the palaces of four heavens." Ancient ruins are marvelous and strange, and cannot be explored in their entirety.

46. The Huang is a major tributary of the Yellow River in modern Qinghai province. The compound of the two rivers represents China's northwestern frontier region, including Dunhuang.

Dazaifu[47]

A poem inspired by Jao's visit to the Enokidera temple near Fukuoka, Japan, where the most famous writer of Chinese verse in Japan, Sugawara Michizane 菅原道真 (845–903), had composed a memorable lament: "Shedding one hundred thousand trails of tears, / All the myriad things are like a dream."

榎寺淒涼一夢中	Enokidera is silent and empty as in a dream.
御兒香帳拂靈風	The emperor's children in scented canopies, brushed by a holy wind.
江楓夜雨歸魂處	The rainswept maples on the river are where the soul returns at night;
合唱怨歌淚點紅	Singing songs of misery in chorus, their teardrops fall crimson.

---

47. 太宰府. *Wenji* 709. One quatrain of three. On Michizane, see Watson, *Japanese Literature in Chinese,* 1: 73–81.

Mourning the Dead at the Peace Park in Hiroshima[48]

The stately pace and regular rhythms of classical Chinese verse, particularly in the pentasyllabic meter, seem proper to a topic as solemn as this one.

一瞬嗟無常	This moment is for grieving at impermanence,
劫灰塞行路	A catastrophe that blocks all paths and roads:
層樓火後茆	Tall buildings became mere weeds after that blaze,
微命草間露	Our insignificant lives like dew upon the grass.
孤炬照千秋	This solitary lamp will burn for one thousand autumns,
一碑睨方怒	Just a glance at the epitaph fills one with indignation.
死者難瞑目	These dead still cannot close their eyes;
誰復蹈此誤	Who again will repeat such a mistake?
荒榛厭人骨	The wild brush devours the bones of men,
森然夜可怖	This stately night is to be feared.
莫言如泡影	Don't say life is like a bubble's reflection:
九京忍重顧	Who can bear to look again at the Nine Capitals of Hades?
我來憑弔久	I have come to mourn for a while,
逝水尚東注	As long as rivers continue to flow on eastward.
佳兵紛未已	Deadly weapons still proliferate without end,
群生那得度	The living things of the earth may not survive.
何以儆後人	How can we warn those to come?
迴車更緩步	Let's turn back and slow the pace a bit.

---

48. 廣島夜弔和平塚. *Wenji* 432–433.

IV

Storms

Some of Jao's poems refer obliquely to the political storms of mainland China, particularly the great famine that occurred during the Great Leap Forward of 1958–1961, and the Great Proletarian Cultural Revolution of 1966–1976. Though Jao was insulated from physical hardship in Hong Kong, he indirectly expresses his concern for the state of his country in a number of poems. For instance, in the series of poems matching the rhymes of the famous third-century poet Ruan Ji on the eve of 1960 on the small island off Hong Kong, Cheung Chau 長洲, Jao imitates the rhymes and the vague sense of foreboding and frustration of Ruan's poems. In a letter Jao once commented on these poems:[49]

> I do not have the complete familiarity of sleeping and eating with these poems, but I have studied and admired the energy of Ruan's work, and think that even after one thousand years, it would still be hard to comprehend all their emotions. I know that Lord Ruan was expert in the *Changes*. After all it is said, "What affliction and sorrow must the authors of the *Changes* have known! ... How well they understood affliction and sorrow, and their causes."[50] This is the true concern of Lord Ruan's own poetic mind. The turmoil and apprehension of the present are even more serious than what Ruan faced. If Lord Ruan were living again today, how could he not write poems? I would not have the temerity to match his rhymes, except that I share something not unlike his sense of apprehension, and so composed these poems accompanying Ruan's.

The other selections here likewise illustrate Jao's indirect representations of political disaster. They generally cannot be dated to any particular events, but are intended to suggest a mood of foreboding or disappointment.

---

49. *Wenji* 484.

50. The set of nine poems on the exiled courtier's frustration, attributed to Qu Yuan and included in the *Chuci* collection.

77

Cheung Chau Collection #16[51]

This poem evokes a vague foreboding through tempestuous imagery, following the model of Ruan Ji. That Jao ostensibly rejects some classic poems of lament and protest from the past is pleasingly paradoxical in a poem that itself is based on the rhymes of a third-century lyric.

狂攘此何世	What age is this to suffer such wild tumult?
海嘯轉強梁	The ocean roar turns violent and fierce.
息我乎沈默	Let me rest awhile sunk in quiet,
攜我乎蒼茫	Accompany me into the vast emptiness.
馮夷欲我歸	Fengyi wants me to return,
風伯挾我翔	The Prince of Winds accompanies me in flight.[52]
過眼如風燈	Vanished in a glance of the eye, like a lamp in the wind,
契闊徒相望	Long separated we gaze toward each other in vain.
寒梅可著花	The winter plums may show off their blossoms,[53]
叢菊幾經霜	But how much frost can chrysanthemums endure?
一念下泉人	When once I think of the poet of the "Underground Springs,"[54]
嘳焉增心傷	I sigh and feel my sorrow double.
滔天如此水	The waters here are flooding high as Heaven,
百變異其常	Transformed a hundredfold their usual height.
君莫賦七哀	Please don't recite "Sevenfold Sorrow,"
我已廢九章	I have already abandoned the "Nine Declarations."[55]

---

51. *Wenji* 466–467. There is an annotated edition of these poems: Chen Hanxi et al., comm., *Xuantang shiji pingzhu: Changzhou ji*.

52. Fengyi is the god of the Yellow River. The Prince of Winds sometimes appears as Pingyi 屏翳.

53. This line alludes to Wang Wei's 王維 poem, "You come from my old home, / And ought to know how it goes there. / In coming days before the silk-rimmed window, / Have the winter plums bloomed or not?" See *Quan Tang shi* 128.1304.

54. Alluding to *Odes* 153, "Xia quan" 下泉, expressing a longing for good government. This poem is also referenced in Wang Can's 王粲 (177–217) famous poem "Sevenfold Sorrow" 七哀, mentioned in the final couplet of this poem.

55. The set of nine poems on the exiled courtier's frustration, attributed to Qu Yuan and included in the *Chuci* collection.

Ancient-Style Verse in Pentasyllabic Meter for My Collection "Ice and Charcoal"[56]

This is one of three poems prefaced to Jao's collection "Ice and Charcoal," which was compiled in 1972 but included older poems as well.

胸次羅冰炭	Ice and charcoal are arrayed in my breast,
南北阻關山	I am imprisoned south and north by mountain walls.
我愁那可解	How can I dispel this sorrow of mine?
一熱復一寒	I feel the heat a while and then the chill.
條風頻布暖	The spring wind comes bringing warmth,
漫云歲已闌	How can one say the year is already done?
宵來爆竹聲	At night comes the sound of firecrackers,
聊以警頹頑	Cautioning me against despair or ennui.

---

56. 自題《冰炭集》五古. *Wenji* 515.

Sleepless Night after Night in Wind and Rain[57]

Jao included these highly suggestive verses in his "Ice and Charcoal" collection.

#1

六載清明不到家	For six years I have not returned home for the Tomb-Sweeping Festival,
石榴花發思逾賒	As pomegranate flowers bloom, my thoughts grow ever more distant.
夢中多少愁風雨	In dreams there are so many tempests of sorrow,
換作商聲遍海涯	If only I could exchange them for an autumn song by the ocean.

#2

何物煮愁能得熟	What thing is it that can boil sorrow until it is cooked all through?[58]
深宵虛負短檠燈	Late into the night I still disappoint the lamp on its low stand.
安排紙筆剛成句	At last when the paper and brush are all arranged, verses newly formed,
穿屋斜風冷可憎	The gale that slices across the house is abominably cold.

#3

燭暗眼昏莫解衣	The lamp dim and vision dazed, I cannot undo my clothes.
薄涼猶似暮春時	This light chill almost feels like late Spring already.
縱吟詩句無人識	Though I recite my verses no one recognizes them.
只有飛蛾撲硯池	Only the passing moths brush past my ink pool.

#4

無花何事雨仍狂	If not the flowers then what is it makes the rain so wild?
樹杪波濤欲撼床	Thundering waves on the treetops begin to shake my bed.
誰向蓬萊斟海水	Who is it pouring the oceans out upon Mount Penglai?[59]
海空水盡是何鄉	After the waters of sea and sky are emptied what place will this become?

---

57. 連夕風雨不寐. *Wenji* 517.

58. The "*Fu* on Sorrow" 愁賦 is attributed to Yu Xin 庾信 (513–581). Only eight lines survive, including: "What can you boil sorrow with until it is cooked through?" See *Yu Zishan jizhu* 1094 (appendix).

59. Penglai is the mythical mountain home of the immortals.

To the Tune of "Sixth-String Air"[60]

Chang Ch'ung-ho's young son caught a silkworm.[61] Ch'ung-ho made a suit to cover it. Whenever someone breathed on it, the silkworm was still asleep without movement, as if unaware of the human world. Alas for this tiny creature, which will expire in spite of the warm feelings around it! I wrote a lyric to comment on this event, following rhymes from *Airs from Beyond the Waves* by Qiao Dazhuang 喬大壯 (1892–1948).

咽風嚙葉	It chokes on the wind and chews up leaves,
姑射餐冰雪	like the Guye spirit that feeds on ice and snow:[62]
捉來呼燈兒女	To catch it, call for a lamp to the boys and girls,[63]
花外無家別	beyond these blossoms it lacks even a home to lose.[64]
襲以雲衣細護	Hold it close in the folds of cloud robes,
鶩度清秋節	we're already past Mid-Autumn Festival.
翠鈿輕鑷	Amid halcyon ornaments and light hairpins
吳蠶睡老	Wu silkworms slumber till they grow old:
惆悵後期先凋髮	after all this worry I will lose my hair first.

* * *

生世何堪作繭	How can you bear to spin out a cocoon in this life?
未死絲難絕	Until you die the thread will not be severed.[65]
吹動六管飛灰	Playing the six flutes till they shoot forth ash,
恨入哀絃撥	regret enters the strings mourning as they are plucked.
莫道人間少暖	Don't say that humanity lacks warmth
除是滄桑竭	till oceans finish changing into mulberry groves.[66]
西風綠減	In the West Wind green shoots decline,
東波紅泛	and red buds are swept up in eastern tides:
淚泣秋早成疊	wax tears shed for Autumn already pile up high.[67]

---

60. 六幺令. *Wenji* 602.
61. Chang Ch'ung-ho 張充和 was one of the friends Jao knew during his year at Yale. An excellent calligrapher, she was the wife of Yale professor Hans Frankel.
62. There was an immortal spirit living on Mount Guye, according to *Zhuangzi* 1.28.
63. Alluding to Jiang Kui's "Music Level with Heaven" 齊天樂 on crickets: "One laughs at the children of the world / Who call for lanterns to catch them under the fence." See Lin, *The Transformation of the Chinese Lyrical Tradition*, 90.
64. A comic reference to Du Fu's poem "No Home to Lose" 無家別 (*Du shi xiangzhu* 7.537).
65. "Thread" is homophonous with "longing" (*si*).
66. A common figure for the dramatic changes that take place over long periods of time.
67. These lines contain echoes of Li Shangyin's "Untitled" poem "Meeting you is hard and leav-

To the Tune of "Gathering Mulberries":
A Gardener in the Hills Gives Me a Narcissus Flower[68]

This particularly compact tune pattern forces Jao to special ingenuity at intertwining imagery of nature's destruction and renewal.

池臺亂後知何許	Who knows, after this tumult, what has become of pools and terraces?
叢石餘青	Green lingers on the cluttered stones.
滿眼新亭	Our gaze is filled by the New Pavilion,[69]
看盡芳菲逐蔕零	We have seen so many bright blossoms reduced to nothing.

* * *

舊山皋澤還佳否	Are the lakes and hills of long ago still as fair as ever?
斜日葦汀	Sun setting on the reeds and islets,
葉澹風櫺	Leaves are pale in the breeze through the latticed windows:
留取冰肌照獨醒	Keep that skin as pure as ice, shining in solitary awareness.[70]

---

ing is hard too." See Liu, *The Poetry of Li Shang-yin*, 66.

68. 採桑子・故山園丁以所植水仙餉予. *Wenji* 580.

69. The New Pavilion was where the elite of the Eastern Jin, who had fled south of the Yangtze River after the conquest of their land, gathered to admire landscapes and feast together. Though enjoying the southern scene, they also commiserated the loss of the North. See *Shishuo xinyu* 2/31.

70. *Zhuangzi* mentions a spirit whose skin is like ice and snow (*Zhuangzi* 1.29), and later "ice-like flesh" becomes a term to praise the pure skin of a lady. Here it seems to describe the narcissus flower (literally *shuixian*, "water immortal"), which is like a pure spirit recalling the beauty of nature in the distant past.

To the Tune of "Rake's Song": An Allegory[71]

The referent of the "allegory" is not specified. Since this lyric belongs to the "Emulating Zhou Collection" completed in 1971, in the midst of the chaos of the Cultural Revolution, we may detect Jao's response to the events in his native country. The poems in this collection were composed during his year visiting at Yale.

江山悲獨往	Through rivers and mountains I journey alone in sadness:
違離久	parted for so long
萬里不成歸	ten thousand miles delay my homecoming.
望越臺百尺	I gaze at the towers of Yue one hundred feet high,
蜀舲千里	the Shu skiffs crossing a thousand miles.
峽風蕭瑟	The wind on the gorges soughs softly,
林影參差	the reflections of the forests ripple here and there.
燕去後	Since the swallows departed,
落花吹滿徑	fallen blossoms are blown across the path,
飛絮盡沾泥	and willow floss is stained by mud.
滄海起波	Waves stir upon the gray-blue seas,
似鳴孤憤	as if crying out in solitary indignation,
暮雲離岫	while evening clouds depart ravines
空惹長悲	stirring up the old sorrow for nothing.

* * *

蒼茫題詩處	Inscribing a poem here in the void,
拋別淚	I wipe away the teardrops of parting
沾滿鳳縷羅衣	that soak the phoenix threads of my gauze robe.
無奈事非人老	It can't be helped that we've grown old,
相見何期	but when will we meet again?
但曉日神州	Only when the sun dawns over the Continent of Spirits[72]
重陰纔改	will the layered shadows first change:
斷鴻江國	a goose lost in the river country,
雪意潛垂	the sense of snow looming overhead.
只恐隱憂攢恨	I only fear this concealed sadness, this long-borne outrage,
沒個人知	will never be known to anyone.

---

71. 風流子・有寄. *Wenji* 637.
72. A term for China itself.

V

Two Rhyme-Matching Sets

The following two sets of poems match the rhymes of famous poetic suites from medieval times. Jao's "Cheung Chau Collection" and "Emulating Zhou Collection" are similar examples where Jao follows the rhymes of a whole group of poems, constructing an original poetic series that can be read both on its own or in tandem with the source.

In both these cases the model poems had already been used for this kind of rhyme matching before. Numerous poets had written series matching Du Fu's "Autumn Meditations," and Jao has in mind a particular attempt to match Tao Yuanming before. But all the complex inspirations and influences are merely background, layers of allusive substructure that do not prevent Jao from conveying his own emotions in these poems.

Matching the Rhymes of Du Fu's "Autumn Meditations"[1]

In a postface to the poems, Jao discusses earlier attempts at matching the rhymes of Du Fu's famous set of eight "Autumn Meditations" 秋興八首.[2] *Most notably, Qian Qianyi* 錢謙益 *(1562–1664) wrote numerous poems of this kind, compiling them together into the collection "Renouncing the Brush"* 投筆集.[3] *Jao mentions that numerous Hong Kong poets have done the same. He also remarks that after finishing the poems, he noticed that they were actually more similar in style to the poems of Li Shangyin, and failed to capture the style of Du Fu. Like Jao's model, this suite consists of eight regulated octets.*

---

1. 秋興和杜韻. *Wenji* 498.
2. *Du shi xiangzhu* 17.1484–1499. For a translation and detailed study, see Mei and Kao, "Tu Fu's 'Autumn Meditations': An Exercise in Linguistic Criticism."
3. For more on these poems, see Lawrence C.H. Yim, *The Poet-Historian Qian Qianyi*.

V | Two Rhyme-Matching Sets

#1

無寐涼飈忽入林	While I try to sleep an icy wind suddenly blows into the forest,
疏櫺燈火助蕭森	Lantern fires sparse on the eaves increase my feeling of desolation.
彌天江海曾傷別	On these Heaven-spanning rivers and seas I once regretted a parting;
漫地風雲詎變陰	Across the earth the stormclouds have not yet darkened fully.
困柳嬌鶯猶喚夢	Trapped in the willows, the dainty oriole calls back a lost dream;
辭枝寒鵲若為心	Departing the branches, a winter magpie feels a twinge of emotion.
義山腸斷非今日	It cannot have been a day like this one that Yishan felt his innards severed;[4]
欲寫秋聲怯夜砧	I'd compare autumn's sound to the fulling block on an anxious night.[5]

---

4. Yishan is Li Shangyin, the innovative poet of untold longing and desire.
5. The repetitive sound of the fulling block evokes the sense of transience.

#2

六曲闌干斗柄斜	Crisscrossing sixfold, the Dipper's handle is askew;
安排筆硯染煙華	Preparing my brush and inkstone, I drench them in misty colors.
唇鬐誰鑄成名馬	Who could forge this mouth, this mane, into a great stallion?[6]
星漢今看有遠槎	Looking out today toward the Milky Way I descry a distant raft.
九縣多方爭豹略	Throughout the Nine Precincts men vie with "Leopard's Stratagems";[7]
萬方一概動羌笳	Across all ten thousand localities the Qiang flutes stir.
胡姬沈醉呼難醒	Tartar maids deep in drink cannot be called awake;[8]
起剔銀釭眼未花	Rising to scrape wax from the silver lamps, my sight is still clear.

---

6. Jao's note identifies the source of this line in a memorial by Ma Yuan 馬援 (14 BCE–41 CE) about horse statuettes he had forged out of bronze from Vietnam (see *Hou Han shu* 24.840). Jao might also have had in mind the contemporary Vietnam War as well.

7. "Leopard's Stratagems" is the name of a chapter in *Six Secret Teachings* 六韜, an ancient military manual.

8. "Tartar maid" is a term for a barmaid, but also an alternative name for the orchid, as Jao observes in a note to this line.

#3

諸天移景澹含輝	The shifting panorama of the skies has a subdued gleam;
上座傳經事已微	The transmission of the Sthavira sutras is already obscure.[9]
荔子偏教樓閣麗	The lychees seem to make these towers and pavilions yet more lovely,
木棉不見鷓鴣飛	While through the cotton trees you cannot see the partridge flying past.
寸丹澆水心餘熱	Though I sprinkle water on my inchlong heart it still burns crimson;
斷碧連山意更違	The hills stand arrayed like emerald shards where the mind goes astray.
往日親朋應眷我	My friends and kin of far-off days must be thinking of me;
籬邊人瘦夕陽肥	This man by the hedge is frail, but the sunset's warming rays are full.

---

9. The Sthavira was one of the early divisions of Buddhism, long preceding its transmission to China. As this line states, its history is not fully understood today.

#4

一葉阽危似累棋	Each lone leaf verges on disaster, precarious as a tower of chess pieces;
淮南枉賦長年悲	Thus the Huainan Sage's unhelpful adage that men "grow sad with age."[10]
紀侯大去還無日	The Marquis of Ji made his great leavetaking" with no return date,[11]
陶令歸來會有時	But Governor Tao had his homecoming right at the appointed time.[12]
關塞他鄉多暝宿	Far from home and beyond the passes we rest at twilight;
江皋余馬苦朝馳	On the riverbanks my steed finds even a morning gallop hard.[13]
賓鴻萬里無消息	Over ten thousand miles no message comes by goose;
林鳥從知有去思	The forest birds, I know, already have a leave-taking in mind.

---

10. *Huainanzi* is quoted thusly in *Yiwen leiju* 88.1507.

11. The Marquis of Ji gave up his office and departed from Ji, never to return, to escape the persecution of the neighboring state of Qi. See *Zuozhuan*, Duke Zhuang, year 4 (*Chunqiu Zuozhuan zhengyi* 8.8a).

12. Tao Qian's famous poem, "The Return!" tells of returning to his farm to live in retirement.

13. This line is a loose adaptation of a couplet from the "Nine Songs": "In the morning I gallop my steed over the riverbanks, / In the evening I cross the western shores." See *Chuci buzhu* 2.66.

#5

雨歇天低峭峭山	When the rain stops the sky looks low over precipitous peaks;
鄉閭指點白雲間	I point to my old village there in the white clouds.
人隨秋水歸群壑	A man should follow the autumn waters back down the ravines;
月帶星河照近關	The moon passing the river of stars shines on the first pass.
叢竹送青還繞屋	The bamboo thickets send along their verdure to surround the house;
金尊浮綠且開顏	Floating green ale lees in a gold goblet, I'll break a smile.
飄殘墜蕊堆庭砌	The falling petals flutter down in a heap on the courtyard steps:
試覓芳蹤向舊班	In search of fragrant traces they look toward their former places.[14]

---

14. Su Shi in his poem "Matching the Rhymes of Qian Mufu" 次韻錢穆父 wrote: "Aged I enter the Mingguang palace, stepping into my former office; / My beard now dyed, how can I sing again 'Yangguan'?" (*Su Shi shiji* 26.1404). Similarly, Jao here imagines the fallen flowers looking back at their positions on the branches.

#6

綠到髡枝最上頭	Fresh green reaches the bald boughs at their highest point,
柳條婀娜不宜秋	The willow branches swaying lithely will not endure autumn.
四時罕變冬仍翠	The four seasons show little transformation, but remain jadegreen in winter.
百卉何知春只愁	The hundred flowers feel nothing themselves, and only spring is melancholy.
去去家山戀落日	As I go further away from my home in the hills I cherish the setting sun,
栖栖南北逐浮鷗	Hastily chasing the airborne gulls southward and northward.
他生未卜今生老	Not yet having divined the next life, in this life I have grown old.[15]
遙認齊煙是九州	Far off through the mists of Qi I recognize all Nine Provinces.[16]

---

15. Adapting a couplet from Li Shangyin's poem "Mawei" on the death of Emperor Xuanzong's concubine Yang Guifei: "From over the seas one only hears of the same Nine Provinces; / Though the next life is not yet divined, this life is already over." Cf. Liu, *The Poetry of Li Shang-yin*, 186.

16. This line is based on Li He's poem "Dreaming of Heaven": "From far away Qizhou is just nine dots of mist." See Frodsham, *Goddesses, Ghosts, and Demons*, 23. Qizhou is one of the Nine Provinces said to make up the entire world, and is the one corresponding to the Middle Kingdom of China.

#7

作稼難邀一溉功	In farming it's hard to demand even a single irrigation;[17]
河山回首日方中	Looking back over rivers and mountains the sun shines directly overhead.
趙岐繫志鳴孤憤	Zhao Qi related his ambition, sounding solitary indignation.[18]
屈子何因歆緒風	Why did Master Qu lament that chill wind from before?[19]
牢落鬢非鴉背黑	My sparse temples are not yet as black as crows' backs;
淺清句共海綃紅	Verses of light and pure fragrance join the red of undersea silks.[20]
江頭多少王孫老	On the riverbanks how many princes have grown old?[21]
最憶滄州此禿翁	Yet we recall best that bald-headed old man on the green isles.[22]

---

17. A "single irrigation" represents a slight effort. Xi Kang 嵇康 (223–263) writes of how the effort of irrigation would be worthwhile even during the drought of Lord Tang, although the plants might ultimately die anyway. See his "Disquisition on Cultivating Long Life" (*Wen xuan* 53.2288).

18. *Mengzi* commentator Zhao Qi 趙岐 (?–201 CE) wrote "I wanted to relate my ambition with brush and ink, aiming to order my thoughts for old age." See "Preface to *Mengzi*" (*Mengzi zhushu* 9a).

19. The "wind from before" is the wind lingering on from autumn and winter, as in the "Nine Declarations" (*Chuci buzhu* 4.129).

20. There was a kind of silk said to be woven by underwater shark people, as in Li He's poem "The King of Qin Drinks Wine" 秦王飲酒: "In ornate towers the voices of jade phoenixes are delicate and alluring, / The undersea silks are patterned with red, the fragrance light and pure. / Yellow maidens trip in their dance, goblets toasting a millennium." See Frodsham, *Goddesses, Ghosts, and Demons*, 44.

21. This line neatly combines allusions to Du Fu's "Lament on the Riverbank" 哀江頭 (*Du shi xiangzhu* 4.329) and "Lament for the Princes' Sons" 哀王孫 (*Du shi xiangzhu* 4.310).

22. Cf. Du Fu, "Facing a Wine Glass at Qujiang" 曲江對酒, "Guarding my feelings I sense the green isles even further away, / In old age I grieve only that I have not yet flicked my collar [and gone into retirement]" (*Du shi xiangzhu* 6.449). The green isles represent retirement outside of public office.

#8

長河望遠自逶迤	Gazing far along the Yellow River winding and unwinding,
漠漠桑田接翠陂	In the remote distance mulberry fields touch halcyon dikes.
北顧窮邊先舞雪	Looking north toward the border, snow flurries dance before me.
南征倦鳥且巢枝	Traveling south a weary bird nests upon a branch.
不愁波淺潛蛟出	I do not worry the waves are so shallow the hidden flood-dragon will appear,
待見山明落照移	But wait to see the mountains clearing as the sun sets beyond.
聽風聽雨黃葉路	I listen to the wind, listen to the rain, as yellow leaves cover the path.
相思華髮正低垂	My hair, blossoming white with longing, now trails low behind.

Latter Ten Poems on Drinking Wine, Written to Match Fang Mizhi's Poems Matching the Rhymes of Lord Tao[1]

This series of poems is modeled on another series by Fang Yizhi 方以智 (1611–1671), identified here by his style name Mizhi. Fang was a highly original thinker of the Ming-Qing transition period. The full title of the original set is "Poems Matching Tao's Rhymes, Composed at Ice Lodge in Wuzhou in the Year Xin mao" 和陶飲酒辛卯梧州冰舍作, a series of twenty poems composed in 1651 when Yizhi had already decided to become a recluse. Jao follows the rhymes of the latter ten poems in the series, that is to say, the rhymes of the latter ten poems in Tao Yuanming's series, which Fang Yizhi had followed previously. But in the content of Jao's poems he refers frequently to Fang's life and writings, so his poems are primarily a response to Fang's matching poems rather than to Tao's originals.[2]

The textual history of the poems is complex. They seem only to be available in a manuscript copy held in the National Palace Museum in Taipei, as well as in a printed copy of Fang Yizhi's collection Fushan houji 浮山後集 *(Latter collection from the floating mountains) held in the Anhui Provincial Museum.[3] As Jao observes, they are poems "scarcely to be seen anywhere in the world" and were nearly forgotten for three centuries after Fang's death. The neglect of these and other writings by Fang was in large part due to his status as a Ming loyalist. In these poems Jao communicates his own sense of identification with Fang's patriotic spirit.*

---

1. 後飲酒十首和方密之用陶公韻. *Wenji* 444–445.
2. For the "Twenty Poems After Drinking Wine," see Hightower, *The Poetry of T'ao Ch'ien*, 124–157.
3. For details and text see Fang Hao, "Fang Yizhi he Tao shi shoujuan ji quanwen," and Ren Daobin, "Fang Yizhi de 'He Tao shi.'"

#1

楚塚發奇書	Strange books appeared from tombs in Chu,
先德而後道	First the "Virtue" and then the "Way."[4]
韓非豈解此	Han Fei could not have understood this,
徒然作喻老	For all that he wrote on "Interpreting *Laozi*."
幾人身佩玉	How many men adorn themselves with jade,
而心如木槁	Yet have hearts that are like deadwood?
天末殘雲飛	At the end of Heaven the cloudwisps fly,
卷舒意自好	Rolling and unrolling just as they like.[5]
蒼翠滿空林	As azure and halcyon hues fill an empty forest,
許興以為寶	The inspirations of experience can serve as my treasure.
秀色落吾詩	That gorgeous scene falls right into my poem,
有懷出繫表	My emotions extend beyond the reach of language.

---

4. Referring to the *Daodejing* excavated from Mawangdui, which reversed the order of the two sections. In the received text they are the "Way" and then "Virtue," as in Duyvendak's rendering *The Way and Its Virtue*.

5. "Rolling and unrolling" are used metaphorically to refer to serving as an official or retiring.

#2

早識東西均	In youth he wrote the *Fashioner of East and West*,[6]
會通此其時	This was a time of ecumenical understanding.
循理寧好異	When following principle, one should not be attracted to the foreign,
體要誰正辭	Who can describe the essential and rectify the terms?
一往古今情	The passions of past and of present have perished alike,
逝者忽如茲	The vanishing away of things is as rapid as this![7]
掩卷興遐思	Thoughts of the remote appear as I roll up the scroll;
夢闌起然疑	Both affirmation and doubt arise as my dream fades.
敗葉亦有廬	Rotting leaves can still be made into a hut,
木立自不欺	Wood stands straight and of itself does not deceive.
茫然觀我生	In this vast universe I examine my own life:
吾道竟何之	Where is it that this way of mine will lead?

---

6. Referring to Fang's deeply original philosophical work, *Dong xi jun* 東西鈞. The title makes a complex pun on the word *dongxi*, which as a compound simply means "things," but is composed of "East" and "West." In Fang's book East and West represent Chinese and Indic thought, respectively. Fang's thought was an original form of syncretism that incorporated Buddhist elements into a Confucian framework.

7. Confucius made this remark while observing the flow of a river. See *Analects* 9/17.

#3

心競水長流	My heart races with the water in the endless current,
何處非人境	What place is there that is not in the human realm?
蒙莊那可炮	Zhuangzi of Meng county could not be roasted;[8]
一睡亦須醒	Once asleep, one still must sometime wake.
群經已糞溺	The various classics might as well be feces and urine,[9]
精義無人領	Since no one can understand their essential meaning.
翻然可無慚	Suddenly enlightened, I am ashamed of my ignorance,
惟有此毛穎	All because of what this brushtip has accomplished.
心苗養其誠	I cultivate sincerity in the green shoots of my heart,[10]
虎變看文炳	In the changing of the tiger's pelt I see resplendent patterns.[11]

---

8. Fang Yizhi wrote the *Zhuangzi* commentary *Yaodi pao Zhuang* 藥地炮莊, "purifying through roasting" the *Zhuangzi* by critiquing its doctrines.

9. This line is referring to the statement in *Zhuangzi* that the Way can be found in all phenomena, even amid feces and urine. See *Zhuangzi* 22.750.

10. According to Fang Yizhi, the "green shoots of the heart" are words (see *Dong xi jun zhushi* 184). With this in mind, the line can be understood as a rephrasing of the "Wen yan" 文言 commentary to *Changes*, hexagram #1, Qian 乾: "Elaborating my words, I found them in sincerity." See *Zhou yi zhengyi* 1.14a.

11. Cf. *Changes*, hexagram #49, Ge 革: "When the gentleman changes like a leopard, the patterns are resplendent" (*Zhou yi zhengyi* 5.20a).

#4

此島繞波濤	This isle is encircled by stormy waves,
飄風偶一至	Stray winds happen to reach it now and then.
枯藤摵且墜	Withered vines quiver and plummet downwards;
蒼天呼豈醉	When I call upon Heaven is it too drunk to answer?[12]
終當待其定	You ought to wait till all is settled in the end;
山海休造次	Mountains and oceans, do not act rashly.
立此不易方	Once this adamant principle is established,
亂流安足貴	Anarchic trends will no longer be valued.
何處冀州原	How far off is the central plain from us now?
沙棠含至味	The ultimate taste is contained within the sand-pear.[13]

---

12. Jao may have in mind a verse by Fang's friend Chen Zilong 陳子龍 (1608–1647): "I would not believe there is truly a Heaven; it seems forever drunk!" See *Chen Zilong shiji* 15.526.

13. A legendary fruit tree mentioned in the *Shan hai jing*, and said to protect from drowning. Here the reference seems to be to Fang's death by drowning. See *Shan hai jing jiaozhu* 2.47 and Strassberg, *A Chinese Bestiary*, 107.

#5

文者天地心	The pattern of words is the heart of Heaven and Earth:
得此心可宅	This heart once obtained, you can reside there.
閉眼思去來	Closing my eyes I ponder what has gone and is to come:
隙馳終無跡	Swiftly as galloping past a tiny crevice, yet ever without trace.
結念在王者	I concentrate my thoughts upon the kingly one
興起須五百	Who appears but once every five hundred years.[14]
漢後閱千年	When a millennium had passed after the Han
史傳尚空白	The annals and records were still blank.
青簡幾成灰	Though green bamboo strips have nearly turned to ash,
黃卷宜珍惜	These yellow scrolls we must cherish and preserve.[15]

---

14. Mencius made this assertion. See *Mengzi zhushu* 4B.11a.

15. Yellow scrolls can refer either to books in general, or to Daoist and Buddhist scriptures.

#6

聲氣終不壞	"Sound and energy can never be destroyed":[16]
中和良可經	A balanced mean is ideal for governance.
其說非耳食	His theories were never like rumors appealing to the ear;
其理豈目成	His principles could not be appreciated at a glance.
自從衰周來	Ever since the Zhou was in decline,
世代紛屢更	The dynasties have undergone countless transformations.
割據如蠻觸	The country has been carved up like Man and Chu,[17]
各自分門庭	Each family confined to its own household gate.
一朝敞神界	If in one day the divine precincts were opened up,[18]
百家忍罷鳴	The hundred schools would still not cease to sing.
品物既流形	Since the species of things vary their forms,[19]
庶得蒼生情	I wish only to understand the feelings of other human beings.

---

16. This is the title of a chapter in Fang Yizhi's *Dong xi jun*.
17. Man and Chu are two countries located on opposite sides of a snail's shell but frequently at war, suggesting the futility and foolishness of human conflicts in *Zhuangzi* 25.891–892.
18. See Tao Qian's "Peach Blossom Grotto" poem, in Hightower, *The Poetry of T'ao Ch'ien*, 254–258.
19. *Changes*, Hexagram #1, Qian: "Clouds move and rain falls, the species of things vary their forms" 雲行雨施，品物流形. Cf. Wilhelm-Baynes, *Book of Changes*, 370.

#7

豪末看此身	I see this body as just the tip of a hair;
高臺起悲風	On a high terrace a sorrowful wind rises.[20]
詩成覺句繁	When the poem is completed I find the lines convoluted,
盡在續貂中	As if I've merely extended a sable with a dog's tail.[21]
作述誠多事	Both creating and transmitting are futile after all;[22]
咫尺意難通	Across each inch the sense is hard to communicate.
太虛如可括	If we can already take the measure of infinite space,
何嘆弨無弓	Why lament there are no bows in the bowcases?[23]

---

20. This verse is nearly identical to a line in Cao Zhi's 曹植 (192–232) "Miscellaneous Poem." See *Wen xuan* 29.1363.

21. Jao uses the same common idiom, humbly characterizing the scope of his ambitions as minimal, in the preface to this series.

22. Cf. *Analects* 7/1.

23. The *Guoyu* describes all the feudal lords making obeisance to the Son of Heaven: although the war chariots were all assembled, they did not ready their armor or weapons, and the "bowcases had no bows, the quivers no arrows" 弨無弓，服無矢. Thus the idiom implies a state of political harmony, when weapons can be put aside. See *Guoyu* 6.243.

#8

求理譬尉羅	Seeking out patterns is like catching birds in a net;
高翔那易得	As they fly high above they are not easy to obtain.
衰柳蔽秋陽	The withered willows hide the autumn sun,
寒氣使人惑	And wintry airs drive men into confusion.
蒼然俯平楚	I look upon the vast and verdant plains,
川途有通塞	Where some routes are open and others closed.
白雲遙可念	The white clouds far off fill me with longing,
招我到江國	They beckon me toward the River Country.[24]
獨鶴下荒原	A solitary crane descends to the desolate plain,
群鴉正嘿嘿	Where the crows go on cawing and cawing.

---

24. The River Country is specifically the Jiangnan region, consisting primarily of the area south of the lower reaches of the Yangtze River.

#9

端坐飛清寒	I sit upright in the chill air swirling all around,
六十羞一仕	Ashamed at sixty never to have served in office.
離披春草外	Past these spring grasses dangling in profusion,
青山即知己	The green hills are my understanding friend.
泛泛弄江鳬	I play with the ducks floating in the river,
淪逸非可恥	This frustration not something to be ashamed of.
玉瑟試彈秋	On a jade zither I try to play autumn tunes,
鏘然思甫里	But that deep echo recalls the hermit of Fuli.[25]
綠窗呵禿筆	In a green-shuttered hovel I thaw my brush with a breath;
洪荒猶可紀	Even primordial chaos can still be recorded.
莫嗟著葉遲	Don't sigh and moan that your leaves have flourished too late,
盤根足棲止	On these twining roots there is a place to perch.
微光參最靈	In the faint light I sense something perfectly divine;
孤燈堪長恃	With this solitary lamp I will be able to sustain myself.

---

25. The hermit of Fuli is Lu Guimeng 陸龜蒙 (?–881), who retired to Fuli in modern Wu 吳 county, Jiangsu.

#10

伯玉師彼愚	Boyu was the teacher of that "Naïve One";[26]
栗里證吾真	He proved his sincerity in Chestnut Grove.[27]
緬焉山水窟	Those grottoes of the hills and rivers are far away,
且賞畫中淳	But I still admire the simplicity of painting.
檻外紛喧攪	Beyond this threshold all is noise and turmoil,
眾卉巧競新	Just so many flowers contending craftily to be original.
智與譎相成	Wisdom and deceit have molded one another:
六譯溯先秦	The "Six Translations" can be traced back to before the Qin.[28]
回首望遠郊	Looking back at the distant suburbs,
而多車馬塵	How many carriages and horses pass in the dust.
耕穫亦云勞	Ploughing and harvesting is already trouble enough;
民生固在勤	The life of the people has always been one of labor.
不飲且如醉	Without drinking I already seem to be intoxicated,
獨與雲水親	Intimate only with the clouds and rivers.
千山無近遠	The thousand peaks cannot be labeled near or far;
疊疊有關津	Every fold and ridge has a pass across it.
地動復天迴	The Earth shakes and Heaven itself revolves;
斜日漫沾巾	In the setting sun I wet my kerchief in vain.
混沌久鑿竅	It was long ago that the seven orifices of Hundun were pierced;[29]
寧有羲皇人	How can the men of Xihuang's age survive today?[30]

---

26. Qu Boyu 蘧伯玉 was a high official of Wei during the Spring and Autumn period, and a model of both service and reclusion. Fang Yizhi's sobriquet was "the Naïve One" 愚者.

27. Chestnut Grove was the place of Tao Qian's retirement, southwest of Jiujiang 九江 city in Jiangxi province. There are a number of allusions to Tao Qian's poems in the lines below, and the whole poem discusses the life of the scholar-recluse, like Tao Qian, Fang Yizhi, and Jao himself.

28. "Six Translations" was the *hao* of Liao Ping 廖平 (1852–1932), a highly original but overly imaginative "New Text" scholar. See Joseph Levenson, *Confucian China and Its Modern Fate: A Trilogy*, Vol. 3, *The Problem of Historical Significance*, 3–15.

29. A sort of creation myth told in *Zhuangzi* 7.309: Hundun, the state of primordial chaos mentioned in the previous poem, had seven orifices pierced to make it like a human being, and died on the seventh day when the process was completed.

30. Xihuang refers to Fuxi, the ancient sage-king who invented writing, and here more generally to the ideal utopia of his prehistoric era.

VI

Alone

This section collects certain of Jao's poems that are especially evocative of the poet's individual reflections while temporarily isolated from society. Though Jao's poems contain extensive evidence of his friendship and associations with other scholars, writers, and artists throughout his life, he does sometimes present himself in solitary aspect as well. Hu Xiaoming writes that while visiting Jao in his study, Jao showed him one of his own paintings entitled, "Journey Through Snow-Covered Mountains" 雪山行. The painting depicted a lone traveler leading a camel through mountains during a heavy blizzard, advancing forward resolutely. Jao pointed to the figure and laughed, saying "That's my self-portrait."[1]

---

1. Zhao et al., *Xuantang shici lungao*, 6.

Cheung Chau Collection #80[2]

This poem follows in a tradition inaugurated by Ruan Ji, the lyric of midnight wakefulness, but with a Buddhist inflection.

我夢向千里	My dream reaches one thousand leagues away,
醒來忽在茲	But when I wake I find myself right here.
一念生三千	A single thought gives rise to a billion worlds;[3]
復與千里期	Again we meet after a thousand leagues' separation.
青天延明月	Blue skies extend into bright moonlight,
欲結新相知	I hope to find some new acquaintance there.
月乎投我懷	The moon lands in my embrace,
解佩而要之	I remove my sash and make a pact with it.
願心如圓月	I'd like my heart to be as the round moon,
遍照去來時	Illuminating every place it comes and goes.

Illustration 6. From a series of *Eight Immortals* (2000).

---

2. *Wenji* 481.

3. According to Tiantai Buddhism, a single thought contains within itself the "trichiliocosm" of one billion (1000³) universes. See, e.g., *Mohe zhiguan* 摩訶止觀, *T* 1911: 46.54a.

To the Tune of "Frosty Leaves Fluttering": On Willows[4]

As the notes indicate, this poem is a pastiche of the late Tang poet Li He.

寒雲腐草	Chill clouds and rotting grasses,
隋堤路	On the Sui dike path[5]
鶯飛心繫江表	orioles in flight, hearts longing for the south of the Yangtze:
即看磷火向人青	When you look upon the will o' the wisps they grow dark,
伴黃昏清悄	and at twilight all is serene.
又颼颼絲絲颶曉	Then the dawn blows in sough by sough and thread by thread;
關河途遠波聲小	The road through passes and rivers is far, the sound of waves faint.[6]
最㾗人	What troubles me most
無奈是漸入蒼茫	is helplessly slipping into the remote haze,
野戍萬里殘照	the light of garrisons fading ten thousand miles away.

                *   *   *

遙望九點齊煙	From far off the province of Qi looks like nine specks of mist:
蓬飄波蕩	the tumbleweed drifting, waves stirred,
脈脈杯瀉難到	capacious waters pouring out untouchable.[7]
吳刀好翦尺天長	Wu knives are fine for cutting out a foot of sky,[8]
寫楚中幽抱	from Chu I write out my concealed ambition.
似走馬	Fast as a galloping horse
千年換了	the fate of a thousand years is transformed.[9]

---

4. 霜葉飛・柳. *Wenji* 613–614.

5. *Ci* lyrics allude frequently to the willow trees planted along the canals by the ill-fated Emperor Yang of the Sui dynasty (r. 604–618), as in Zhou Bangyan's lyric to the tune of "Prince of Lanling." See *Qingzhen ji jiaozhu* 31.

6. Adapting a line from Li He's "Songs of the Bronze Immortal Bidding Farewell to Han" 金銅仙人辭漢歌: "Weicheng was already far off, the sound of its waves faint." See Frodsham, *Goddesses, Ghosts, and Demons*, 54.

7. Here Qi is the central one of the Nine Provinces of the universe, or the Middle Kingdom itself. From Li He's "Dreaming of Heaven" 夢天: "From far away Qizhou is just nine dots of mist, / An ocean of water may be poured into a cup." See Frodsham, *Goddesses, Ghosts, and Demons*, 23.

8. From Li He's "Verses on Being Presented with a Length of Summer Cloth from a Hermit of Mount Luofu" 羅浮山人與葛篇: "I'd like to cut out a foot of sky out of the river Xiang." See Frodsham, *Goddesses, Ghosts, and Demons*, 71.

9. This line again borrows from Li He's "Dreaming of Heaven": "Yellow dust and pure waters below the three mountains, / one thousand years transformed swiftly as a galloping horse."

幺絃無此淒涼調　　Even on the lute's shortest string you cannot play this mournful tune.
看舊徑　　　　　　Look down the old path
吹綿處　　　　　　　where willow catkins blow past
驚問桓溫　　　　　　　and a startled Huan Wen asked:
緣攀多少　　　　　　　　how far around these trees can I reach now?[10]

---

10. Huan Wen made this remark when he saw that willows he had planted had already grown to a circumference of ten handspans, adding, "If trees can change so quickly, how can men bear it [the passage of time]?" See *Shishuo xinyu* 2/55.

To the Tune of "Little Hills Doubled": On Plum Blossoms[11]

A celebration of the refined sense of sadness implicit in the plum blossom.

梅蕊猶含隔歲春	The pistils of the plum still bear the scent of last year's spring:
東風鉤夢起	The East Wind lifts away that dream
了無痕	without any trace.
替人呵護有春雲	To watch over us there are the spring clouds;
淒絕處	What a desolate place where
野水照黃昏	twilight is reflected in remote streams.

* * *

休更說寒溫	Don't speak to me anymore of cold and warmth.
池萍經雨碎	The duckweed in the pool is dispersed by rain,
易消魂	and it's easy to lose your soul here.
碧桃已是嫁東君	Azure peach blossoms are married off with the Lord of the East.[12]
無人管	But no one is concerned,
燈火掩閒門	and lanterns burn by the tranquil gate.

---

11. 小重山 • 江梅. *Wenji* 569.
12. The "Lord of the East" is the East Wind.

Seeing the Moon in the Hills[13]

This poem celebrates the intuitive understanding represented by a glimpse of the moon between forested hills late in the evening. It belongs to the "Mont Blanc Collection" composed to the rhymes of Xie Lingyun while Jao was traveling with Demiéville.

昔年搗藥窟	In a grotto where once an elixir was concocted,[14]
寂寞抱高岑	All alone the moon touches the high ridge.
得地恐石田	Could I obtain this land, I fear the fields would be stony.
窺天只泥沈	Observing Heaven I simply sink into the mud.
初陽不到處	The first light of spring does not reach here,
終古惟窮陰	Since antiquity it has been a place of extreme darkness.
勞君苦登頓	What an effort you have made to climb up there,
芳意一何深	An exquisite conception that is indeed profound.
人力眞勝天	Human power truly surpasses that of heaven,
繁星復如林	The stars look numerous as a forest again.
形與影競馳	Body and shadow race together,
何以寧此心	But how to calm this heart?
已知即無知	Understanding is the same as lack of understanding:
所尙在靈襟	What matters is that inside the spirit-lapel.[15]
空山不見人	No one to be seen in these empty hills:[16]
有月惜無琴	There is a moon but I regret having no qin to play.

---

13. 山中見月. *Wenji* 392. To the rhymes of "Wanchu xishe tang" 晚出西射堂 by Xie Lingyun (*Xie Lingyun ji jiaozhu* 82).

14. According to legend Chang'e 嫦娥 stole an elixir of immortality and enjoyed her eternal life on the moon.

15. "Inside the spirit-lapel" refers to the heart.

16. This is the first line of Wang Wei's famous quatrain "Deer Fence" 鹿柴 (*Quan Tang shi* 128.1300).

To the Tune of "Wu men": Matching the Rhymes of Wang Yisun's "Sense of Snow"[17]

In this rhyme-matching poem, Jao follows the subject matter of his model's poem as well, describing the cold desolation of a winter snowstorm. The model is a ci *lyric by thirteenth-century poet Wang Yisun* 王沂孫, *compiler of the anthology "Beyond the Flowers."*

欲旦延陰	When dawn approaches dark shadows remain,
先瞑未昏	and it is already dark before the dusk,
殘日高樓倦倚	weary of facing the setting sun in this high tower;
怕成朔淒風	I fear that the piercing north wind will come,
氣清如此	the air is so crisp.
已過傷秋冷落	The time of grieving for autumn's desolation has passed,
睇遠路	looking back on the long road
滄波彌雲水	where endless waves roil the clouds and rivers.
早殘蕙艸	Already the angelica perish:
瘞花綴玉	flowers are buried beneath jade snowflakes
如綿初墜	like willow catkins just fallen.

* * *

荒致	This scene of emptiness:
更誰似	what does it resemble?
看倒影椒塗	I see inverted reflections on the pepper path,[18]
頓生春意	abruptly creating a sense of spring.
恨水闊山孤	I mourn the wide waters and solitary peaks,
漫勞遐睇	striving in vain to peer far off.
擬把瓊枝畫好	I'd like to paint the crystalline branches perfectly,
暫換取	and exchange for a while
芳菲生塵世	that pure fragrance returning to the dusty earth.
只剩得	But all that's left
無限癡寒	is endless confounding cold
化作梨花鋪地	which transforms into pear blossoms carpeting the earth.

---

17. 無悶・和中仙雪意. *Wenji* 603.

18. In early poetry fragrant plants often modify various objects to indicate their worth. In this case the source is Cao Zhi's "Rhapsody on the Goddess of the Luo River": "She treads in the strong pungency of pepper-plant paths, / Walks through clumps of pollia, scattering their fragrance." See Knechtges, *Wen xuan*, 3:361.

To the Tune of "Silk Fishing Line" [19]

There is a short poem from India that goes: "Since you have been gone, / Each day is like a year. / While you were here, / each year was like a day." I was profoundly moved by it, and wrote this to elaborate on that idea.

不年不日	Not just one year, not just one day:
明璫低想眉嫵	I pine for her sparkling earrings and other charms.
記取惜分	I recall our tender parting,
熨水黏絮	willow floss clinging to calm waters;
人暗許	I tacitly promised
動寶箏玉柱	To play a jeweled lute on its jade fret.

* * *

空朝暮	Frustrated morning and night:
隔門前遠路	Separated by the road leading far from the gate,
愁君一去	I feel melancholy since you left
茫茫江海難遇	as we cannot meet across the vastness of river and sea.
霎時俊侶	The fair companion of an instant,
徒念相逢處	futile dreams of our onetime rendezvous.
紅濕胭脂雨	Drenched in a torrent of rouge
桃欲語	the peach blossoms would like to speak:
問舊遊記否	Do you still remember that place we used to go?[20]

---

19. 垂絲釣. *Wenji* 636.

20. There was a popular medieval story about two men named Liu Chen 劉晨 and Ruan Zhao 阮肇 who visited a magical land where they met two maidens. See Chan, "A Tale of Two Worlds: The Late Tang Poetic Presentation of the Romance of the Peach Blossom Font."

Late Stirrings for Hsüan-t'ang[21]

This relatively plainspoken poem in two stanzas (distinguished by different rhymes) sets forth Jao's (Hsüan-t'ang's) determination to enjoy life through the medium of scholarship and art.

#1

高樓俯大荒	From a high tower I look upon the great wastes,
浮雲任變化	Where floating clouds surrender to change and transformation.
隱几萬卷書	I lean over the table with my myriad scrolls of books,
亦足藏天下	Which are sufficient to conceal the entire world.[22]
茗搜文字腸	While drinking tea I search the entrails of language,[23]
潔宮守智舍	In a pristine palace I guard a shrine to wisdom.
浩歌送北風	With glad song I'll send off the North Wind;
俛焉俟來者	And bowing low await those to come.

#2

天墜故不憂	Because Heaven disposes, I will not be sad;[24]
四十心未動	At forty my heart has not yet stirred.[25]
極目寒波外	Extending my gaze beyond the chill waves,
九州紛總總	I see the Nine Provinces bustling with life.
且酌杯深淺	For now I'll pour a glass, whether deep or shallow,
莫問鼎輕重	And not ask if the tripods are light or heavy.[26]
有人夜持山	Someone secreted away a mountain in the night;
案上長供奉	I keep it on my desk to pay it homage.[27]

---

21. 選堂晚興. *Wenji* 418.
22. Zhuangzi writes that if you hide a mountain in a pool, believing it secure, even then someone may come at night and take it away from you. Even if you conceal the entire world in the entire world, you will not escape the inevitable depredations of time. See *Zhuangzi* 6.243.
23. This adapts a line from a poem by Huang Tingjian 黃庭堅 (1045–1105): "While drinking tea I search for words to echo in my wizened entrails." See *Shangu neiji shizhu* 13.251.
24. See the *Book of Changes*, "Appended Statements": "[One who has mastered the *Changes*] can rejoice in Heaven, understand his destiny, and so be free of care." Cf. Wilhelm-Baynes, 295.
25. Mencius said, "Now that I am forty I do not stir my heart." See *Mengzi zhushu* 3A.7a.
26. When a viscount of Chu asked if the tripods were heavy or light, large or small, Wang Sunman 王孫滿 replied that the issue was not the size of the tripods but whether the ruler possessed virtue or not. See *Zuozhuan*, Duke Xuan, year 3.
27. Returning to the *Zhuangzi* passage mentioned above, Jao playfully suggests that he is indifferent to time's depredations, and will simply enjoy observing them from his study.

VII

On Painting

Jao is a highly accomplished and prolific painter. His painting in various genres can be summarized no more easily than his poetry, though he certainly excels in landscapes and Buddhist subjects. Jao has consistently integrated poetry into his paintings and vice versa, whether by composing his own quatrains or other inscriptions for paintings, or by alluding to and recreating visual imagery in his poems. The synthesis of poetry and painting is calligraphy, and in fact, Jao is even more famous as calligrapher than as painter.

Jao has elaborated on the shared principles of poetry and painting in a scholarly essay.[1] He quotes from a poem by Yang Jian 楊簡 (1141–1226): "The inkstone is Heaven's Pool; the ink the Clouds of the Mystery; the brush is a dragon; and riding the dragon is some divinity, I know not what!"[2] Jao also reflects on the fundamental inspiration of Chan Buddhism for both poetry and painting, and concludes, "Since painting is a silent form of poetry, how can painting ever depart from Chan itself?"[3] For Jao, the wordless concentration of painting is a form of religious meditation.

In another essay focusing on the relationship between the ci lyric and painting, Jao borrows the concept of "transposition d'art" from Théophile Gautier (1811–1872).[4] He observes that even though poetry and painting are fundamentally different arts, it is always possible to "transpose" elements from one into the other. Part of the pleasure of the following poems is tracing Jao's own transpositions from the medium of painting.

---

1. "Shi hua tong yi" 詩畫通義, in *Rao Zongyi ershi shiji xueshu wenji*, 18: 342–346.
2. Ibid., 18.342.
3. Ibid., 18.345.
4. Ibid., 18.347–362.

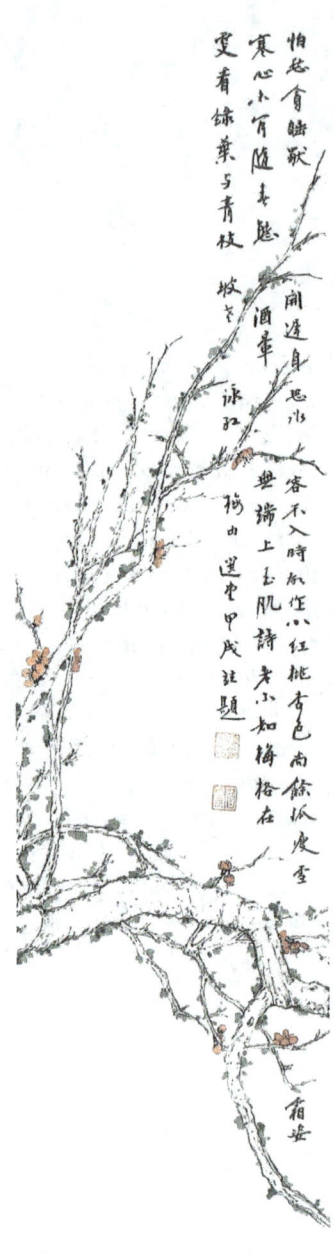

Illustration 7.
Plum Blossom in Double-Line Style (1994).

To the Tune of "Sparse Shadows":
On a Painting of Plums for Li Fengbo[5]

Plums have long been a popular subject for ci *lyrics. This tune pattern was created by Jiang Kui, a.k.a. "White Stone."*

縞衣解佩	Undoing the clasp of the satin robe,
問薄寒翠袖	I ask, with the light chill on the halcyon sleeve,
天遠歸未	have you returned from as far as Heaven itself?
欲切春雲	I want to cut a piece of spring cloud,
重補香瘢	to heal again the fragrant wound:[6]
孤山漫負深意	the lonely mountain lacks a deeper meaning.
偏攀入小窗橫幅	As you climb across the precarious windowsill
終莫信	don't come to believe
扶春不起	that you cannot raise up the Spring;
歎路遙	Sigh that the road is far
竹際溪邊	to the bamboo beside the stream:
冷落買栽無地	no place to plant you there in the stillness.

* * *

暗憶	Remembering faintly
黃昏省識	how we met at twilight,
只瀟灑一枝	just a single lovely branch—
斜照荒水	Reflecting askance deserted waters,
危涕春風	weeping profusely in the spring wind,
瘦損何郎	there was that thin Master He:
東閣早無清致	but the East Court early lost its pristine charm.[7]
翻勞白石工傳恨	Only White Stone strove to pass on that sense of regret,
更樹壓	the trees swaying further
寒湖波碎	where waves break on the chill lake.
等絮飛	Wait till the catkins fly,
不到江南	not ever reaching the Southland:
誰伴濃斟淺醉	who will pour me a glass, share a brief intoxication?

---

    5. 疏影・題梅為李鳳坡. *Wenji* 571.

    6. This line is based on a *ci* on fallen plum blossoms by Wu Wenying 吳文英 (c. 1200–1260), to the tune of "Gaoyang Terrace" 高陽臺. See *Mengchuang ci quanji jianshi* 3.266.

    7. "East Court" refers to He Xun 何遜 (480–520), who wrote poems on plum blossoms, as mentioned in Du Fu's poem "Matching Pei Di's Poem About When We Ascended the East Pavilion of Shuzhou to Send off a Visitor, and the Plums Were in Early Bloom" 和裴迪登蜀州東亭送客逢早梅. See *Du shi xiangzhu* 9.781.

Quatrains Inscribed on Paintings[8]

Jao compiled this series of quatrains to the same rhyme while living in Singapore. He was on the faculty of the National University of Singapore from 1968 to 1973, though he also traveled part of that time, including his visit to Yale in the academic year 1970–1971. These are quatrains Jao composed for his own paintings, all to the same rhymes (shi 詩 – zi 姿 – shi 時), imitated here as rhyme – gleam – time.

#1

天含神霧水如詩　　Under Heaven's divine mist the water is like a rhyme:
湖草尋常祇弄姿　　As ever the lake plants show off their gleam.
猶是荻花楓葉地　　It is still the abode of silver grass and maple leaves,
夕陽無語雁來時　　Twilight brings the silence of geese's nesting time.

#2

坐對蒼茫始詠詩　　Facing the azure haze I prepare to make a rhyme.
落花逝水夢生姿　　Blossoms fall, rivers run, and a dream begins to gleam.
臨風自拂鵝溪絹　　In the breeze the silk of Goose Creek is swept clean.[9]
添個蜻蜓立片時　　I'll paint a dragonfly to stand there for a time.

#3

耶溪小艇欲追詩　　From a skiff on the Ruoye Creek pursuing a rhyme:[10]
荷葉荷花十里姿　　Ten miles along the lotus leaves and lotus blossoms gleam.
若見宓妃憑問訊　　If you see the goddess Fufei could you ask her when
碧梧可有鳳棲時　　On paulownia trees the phoenix has its perching time?[11]

#4

去水漣漪合入詩　　The ripples of the passing stream join in my rhyme,
波瀾紙上動風姿　　On the canvas too the billows churn and gleam.
湖光四面寬如許　　The light upon the lake extends to the far horizons,
商略殘陽欲墜時　　The flickering sun prepares to set around this time.

---

8. *Wenji* 555–557.

9. The silk from Goose Creek in Sichuan province was famous for its quality and during the Song dynasty was popular as a medium for calligraphy and painting.

10. Ruoye Creek in Shaoxing was said to be the place where Xi Shi, the Han dynasty beauty, had bathed.

11. Referencing Du Fu, "Autumn Meditations" #8, *Du shi xiangzhu* 17.1497.

#5

西風卷地忍拋詩	While the West Wind sweeps the plain, how can I discard my rhyme?
南雁飛來媚遠姿	As geese arrive from the south, their far-flung feathers gleam.
寫得鴛鴦難嫁與	Drawn thus even lovebirds would not appear conjoined,
虧它涂抹費移時	For each daub of paint uses too much of their time.

#6

老圃瓜疇且種詩	In this old melon patch I'll seed my rhyme,
苔滋雨足樹凝姿	Planting it amid mossy banks and raindrops' gleam.
華胥潑墨渾成黑	A spray of ink from the Huaxu dreamland turns all to black;[12]
春在雲山懵懂時	The cloud-covered mountains are misty with springtime.

#7

一川雨歇暮催詩	When the river of rain is dried up, evening impels a rhyme:
鼓吹鳴蛙豹隱姿	While the frogs pipe and drum, the leopard hides its gleam.
畫境人家誰會得	Who is there who understands the realm of painting?
登樓好是去梯時	Only he who threw away the ladder to supply more time.[13]

#8

虛堂密雨可藏詩	In this forgotten, rainswept chamber hides a rhyme:
雨洗叢篁見妙姿	When the reeds are washed you see their magic gleam.
又報春江添一尺	They report the spring river has added another foot;
觀瀾徙倚夕陽時	Linger to watch the ripples pass at evening time.

#9

開圖道是無聲詩	Opening a scroll you would call it a silent rhyme.
投葦鴻飛亦駐姿	When swans descend to the reeds, you try to catch that gleam.
一路霜林看不盡	I can't watch enough the road passing through frosty groves,
雲山萬里葉黃時	Over miles of cloudy hills the leaves yellowing in time.

#10

林塘恍似夢中詩	This forested pond is almost like some dreamy rhyme,
況是春江雨後姿	Even more so with spring rain on the riverbanks agleam.
隱隱青山如舊識	Dimly in the distance green hills are like old friends,
夕陽人在倚樓時	For sharing sunset rays upon the tower at this time.

---

12. "Huaxu" is a utopian world described in *Liezi jishi* 2.41.

13. According to the *Gu hua pinlu* 古畫品錄, the painter Gu Junzhi 顧駿之 would climb a tower and throw away the ladder to focus on his painting, rarely seeing his wife and children. See *Taiping yulan* 751.3a.

#11
一幅天然沒字詩　　A perfectly natural and utterly wordless rhyme:
春回草木換新姿　　Spring returning to the plants renews their gleam.
窗前打稿奇峰在　　Writing lines before the window, marvelous peaks stand out;
剪取湖雲拂岸時　　Beside the lakeshore I snip the cloudwisps out in time.

#12
縷縷爐煙處處詩　　Thread upon thread of hearth smoke everywhere a rhyme,
紫禽柳巷作吟姿　　Purple fowl in willow lanes chirp tunes that gleam:
芭蕉猶滴心頭雨　　The plantain leaves still drip away innermost heart's rain,
看放春晴幾許時　　I wonder when the sky will clear and come springtime?

#13
天巧施來苦費詩　　Heaven-sent artifice bestows a painstaking rhyme,
西山遠處澹無姿　　Far off the western hills look wan without much gleam.
眼前佳景君能說　　Could you put in words this splendid scene before us?
一抹微雲吐月時　　A daub of cloud casting out the moon from present time.

Illustration 8. *Trees by the Stream* (1980s). Inscribed with Quatrain #11.

#14

人間誰道苦於詩	Who could claim that living is harder than composing rhyme?
筆底河山宛異姿	At brush's tip the mountains and rivers show a brand new gleam.
欲為漣娟題秀句	I'd like to inscribe some perfect line for such a sinuous scene,
黃昏汐退月生時	When the moon rises at twilight, the tide's receding time.

#15

割愁有劍可裁詩	There is a sword for excising pain to make a rhyme.
海畔尖山聳玉姿	On the seashore the pointed peaks tower with jadelike gleam.[14]
坡老應驚秋未改	Old East Slope would be startled that the autumn has not yet gone.
微波髣髴洞庭時	These faint ripples do resemble Lake Dongting at that time.[15]

#16

揀盡寒枝冷似詩	I gather up cold branches, branches cold as rhyme:[16]
江深春淺澹含姿	The river is deep, but spring is shallow and withdraws its gleam.
莫嫌詩淚無多滴	Don't worry that there are not enough teardrops in these poems;
猶及紛紅駭綠時	Just wait till red blossoms scatter with green leaves at one time.

#17

懶向人前舉好詩	Diffident now to present to strangers any decent rhyme,
看花如史忽移姿	I see the flowers are like history, adding or losing their gleam.
春光墜地誰收整	Who can put in order the spring sunlight on the ground?
莫待湖陰綠滿時	Don't wait for green to fill the reflections on the lake this time.

#18

薔薇無力女郎詩	The roses are as weak and helpless as a girlish rhyme;[17]
皓月梢頭想夕姿	The brilliant moon on the treetop recalls some twilight gleam.
暗柳蕭蕭星冉冉	Dark willows whistling, stars beginning to glisten;
描成天上斷腸時	I'll sketch the heavenly image of this broken-hearted time.

---

14. This couplet recalls a quatrain by Liu Zongyuan 柳宗元 (773–819). See *Quan Tang shi* 351.3932.

15. East Slope is Su Shi, who wrote a "Rhapsody on the Aspect of Spring at Dongting Lake" 洞庭春色賦. See *Su Shi wenji* 1.11.

16. The first half of this line is a direct quotation from a lyric by Su Shi: "To the tune of 'Bu suan zi': Written While Lodging at Dinghuiyuan in Huangzhou" 卜算子·黃州定慧院寓居作. See *Dongpo yuefu* A.24.

17. Yuan Haowen 元好問 wrote of lyricist Qin Guan: "Set Han Yu's line from 'Mountain Rocks' against these, / And it becomes clear, Qin Guan's is girlish poetry." See Wixted, *Poems on Poetry*, 184.

#19

少日山齋聽說詩	When I was young in my mountain studio, I heard of a rhyme:
秋風微月雁沈姿	Autumn wind and faint moon, geese's vanishing gleam.
老來筋力能安處	As age encumbers my body, where may I rest?
看取波平似掌時	When waves are level as the palm of my hand, not till that time.

#20

四十年間千首詩	In the span of four decades one thousand poems to rhyme:
支公神駿足雲姿	Lord Zhi's divine stallions displayed a cloudlike gleam.[18]
金丹九轉工裁句	I craft nine transformations of gold and cinnabar to make a verse,[19]
偏愛山程水驛時	All the fonder of this mountain-roaming, river-lodging time.

#21

獨好杯中日日詩	I love above all the drink in the cup and a daily rhyme;
茗搜文字更增姿	Searching for words in the drinking of tea only deepens its gleam.[20]
玉璜天際誰梳洗	Who can brush clean that jade pendant at the edge of heaven?
奈此夜山片月時	Let alone this crescent moon in the mountains of the night-time.

#22

屏山圍處合鏖詩	Where the mountain screen surrounds, they strive to make out a rhyme.
瓶裏胡姬絕世姿	The tartar maid inside the vase has a world-surpassing gleam.[21]
寄語玉人休勸酒	I'll send a word to the jade beauty not to press more drink on us.
柳花不似故園時	These willow flowers are not as in the old garden at that time.

#23

泉聲帶雨欲搜詩	In the voice of springs and rain I'd like to hunt for a rhyme.
咫尺陰晴已易姿	Shade and sun are only an inch apart, so easily exchanging their gleam.
試向曹溪分一滴	I'd like to share a drop with the master of Cao Stream;[22]
萬山蕭寺聞鐘時	When a bell in the myriad-mountain temple tolls the time.[23]

---

18. The monk Zhi Dun 支遁 (314–366) was fond of raising fine horses, but did not ride them himself. When someone asked him about it, he said he simply admired the "divine stallions." See *Shishuo xinyu* 2/122.

19. The "nine transformations" compare the writing of a poem to Daoist alchemy.

20. This adapts a line from a poem by Huang Tingjian: "While drinking tea I search for words to echo in my wizened entrails." See *Shangu neiji shizhu* 13.251. Cf. "Late Stirrings for Hsüan-t'ang" above.

21. "Tartar maid" is an alternative name for the orchid, and the flower in the vase is a common image for a beautiful woman. In Chinese *ping* ("vase") can also mean "wine bottle."

22. Cao Stream was where the Sixth Patriarch of Chan Buddhism, Huineng 慧能 (638–713), expounded the Way.

23. The temple is literally a "Xiao temple," a way of referring to Buddhist temples after Xiao Yan 蕭衍 (464–549), Buddhist founder of the Liang dynasty.

#24

林棲坐詠偈兼詩	Perching in the forests, I sit to recite a gāthā and a rhyme;
煙鎖橫塘夕變姿	The mists hover over Hengtang, the evening changes its gleam.
雨過柴扉人跡少	Rain passes the hedge gate, and human footsteps are scarce.
萬花一鳥不鳴時	A single bird amid ten thousand flowers does not call out this time.

#25

雁字寥天那遜詩	A line of geese in the boundless sky is equal to a rhyme;
白蘋風裏綠楊姿	White clover in the breeze and green willows' gleam.
小船搖曳歸何處	Your little boat, rocked and rolled, whither will it return?
指點頹陽沒水時	Just point to where sun fades into water around this time.

#26

不仗春風與補詩	Do not rely on the spring wind to supply a rhyme:
無人賞處有幽姿	Where no one is around to admire it there is some hidden gleam.
姚黃魏紫皆陳調	Yao Yellow and Wei Violet are now just old melodies;[24]
最念亭亭玉立時	I think most of how the peonies stand straight and jadelike every time.

#27

疏星歷歷最宜詩	A few stars glinting bright are best of all for a rhyme;
澗水無聲瀉悄姿	The water of the stream is a voiceless torrent with a secret gleam.
隔箇窗兒看更澈	Looking from the other side of the window you see more clearly
四圍秋色未寒時	The aspect of autumn on all sides approaching wintertime.

#28

長薄清川美似詩	Luscious growth on the pristine river is lovely as a rhyme;
傍崖幽草自成姿	The hidden grasses all along the cliff have their own sort of gleam.
茅茨可有倪高士	There could be a Recluse Ni somewhere amid the reeds and caltrops,[25]
秋到灘平水落時	When autumn reaches the level shores, the waters' receding time.

#29

鯤化為鵬意比詩	The Kun fish turned into a Peng bird—a story strange as rhyme;[26]
莊生漫衍故多姿	Master Zhuang had an eccentric mind of manifold gleam.
山河大地都如許	The mountains and rivers of the Earth are like this too;
收拾賦心入定時	Collecting my heart for composition I enter meditation on time.

---

24. Two precious types of peonies from the Song dynasty.
25. The Chan-inspired painter Ni Zan 倪瓚 (1306–1374).
26. The transformation of the gigantic Kun into the equally enormous Peng is the mysterious allegory that opens *Zhuangzi* 1.1.

#30
寂寥人外可無詩	Pure tranquility beyond the human is not beyond all rhyme:
手摘星辰布仙姿	You can gather up the constellations in your hand, and spread their immortal gleam.
肘下諸峰爭起伏	The peaks beneath your elbows contend in their peaks and valleys,
迷離宛溯上皇時	A wild confusion as if we were back in the High God's time.[27]

#31
畫史常將畫喻詩	Historians of painting often represent it by a rhyme;
以詩生畫自添姿	Producing art by poetry will furnish a brighter gleam.
荒城遠驛煙嵐際	At a frontier post in a remote town, at the border of misty crags,
下筆心隨雲起時	Wield your brush as your heart follows along the clouds in time.

#32
畫家或苦不能詩	Some painters may regret they cannot write a rhyme;
嫫母西施各異姿	But Mother Mo and Xi Shi each have a distinct kind of gleam.[28]
物論何曾齊不得	Discoursing on things, why not make them out to be identical?[29]
且看一畫氤氳時	Just look at this painting of a mist-beshrouded time.

#33
何當得畫便忘詩	Because you've obtained a painting should you forget to rhyme?
搔首無須更弄姿	No need to keep scratching my scalp to polish its gleam.
惟有祖師彈指頃	For a patriarch of Chan all this is just a snap of the fingers.
神來筆筆華嚴時	When spirit moves, every brushstroke writes again of Flower Garland time.[30]

---

27. "High God" is another name for Fuxi, the primordial ruler.
28. Mother Mo was the fourth wife of the Yellow Emperor and famously ugly, while Xi Shi was a celebrated beauty of the Spring and Autumn era.
29. Playing on the title of the *Zhuangzi* chapter "Disquisition Proving That Things Are the Same" 齊物論.
30. I.e., Huayan or Avataṃsaka Buddhism.

More Quatrains Inscribed on Paintings[31]

These quatrains do not share the same rhyme scheme and were originally composed for various paintings at different times. Joined together as they are in Jao's collected works, though, they seem unified by the consistent point of view of their author.

#1

路入深林不計層	The road enters the deep woods, so far you cannot count the layers;
好雲表秀復藏棱	Fine clouds display the blooms then hide the edges of clouds.
諸峰清苦巨然筆	Those peaks look serenely aloof under Juran's brush:[32]
商略山居學老僧	I'll prepare a mountain abode like that old monk.[33]

#2

石洞玲瓏地勢殊	The stony cave has a resonant ring, as the shape of the earth is uneven.
丹林黃葉隱仙癯	In crimson groves and yellow leaves, there hides a lithe immortal.
扁舟載得浮萍去	My flat-bottomed skiff can bear away the floating duckweed,
浩蕩無心到具區	Riding stormy seas without particular motive all the way to Juqu.[34]

#3

畫裡磵阿可卜居	One could divine a residence in the painting's gullies and hilltops;
一丘一壑足三餘	One hill and one valley are enough to satisfy the "three residues."[35]
臨流獨欲思濠濮	Looking into the current, I alone would like to think of Hao and Pu.[36]
林水雲山勝道書	Forested rivers and cloud-covered hills are better than Daoist treatises!

#4

蕭寥涼樹雜尖風	Cool trees in a quiet place, a sharp breeze passing by,
懶瓚心情或許同	The feelings of Lazy Jade perhaps were similar.[37]
殘墨自磨還自試	I polish the traces of ink by myself and try again.
亂雲飛下不成峰	Chaotic cloudbursts sail down not ever forming a whole peak.

---

31. 題畫絕句. *Wenji* 559–561. A few quatrains have been omitted.

32. Juran 巨然 was a painter from the Five Dynasties era.

33. Jiang Kui wrote: "A few peaks serene and aloof / Prepare for the twilight rain to come." Cf. Lin, *The Transformation of the Chinese Lyrical Tradition*, 201.

34. Juqu is another name for Lake Tai, on the border of Zhejiang and Jiangsu provinces.

35. "One hill, one valley" represents reclusion, as in *Shishuo xinyu* 9/53. For "three residues" see Introduction.

36. The Hao and Pu rivers are two of the sites where Zhuangzi roams and reflects on life in *Zhuangzi*.

37. Lazy Jade (Lanzan 懶瓚) was a monk who lived on Mount Heng 衡山 in the Tang dynasty.

#5

風吹雨洗勝於藍	The wind blows and the rain washes, bluer than indigo.[38]
一葉搖秋百不堪	One leaf sways the autumn, the other hundred cannot bear it.
自有客懷清絕處	I start to feel a traveler's longings, where everything is absolutely serene.
斷霞疏柳似江南	The splintered cloudwisps and scattered willows are just as in Jiangnan.

#6

獨往深情孰與俱	Lone wandering with profound feeling: who is there to share it?[39]
山如飛白樹如蕪	These hills seem made by "flying white," the trees plentiful as weeds.[40]
亂峰和夢渾難辨	But tangled peaks and dreams are now hard to tell apart.
入座春風筆不枯	With spring wind arriving in place, my brush will not grow brittle.

#7

東風力可護花殘	Can the East Wind's might guard these blossoms from decay?[41]
似夏長年忽歲闌	What seems like an eternal summer is suddenly ended.
且折一枝聊寄與	I'll snap off a spray of plum and send it over to you,
教人知道有春寒	To let people know that the springtime can be cold too.

#8

群山遠勢與湖平	The shape of the mountains far off is level with the lake;
老屋疏林倚晚晴	Old houses lonely in the forest only clear at dusk.
欲為米家祛懵懂	I'd like to clear up the foggy haze of the Mi family,[42]
楚天雲霧一江清	The clouds and mist of Chu skies become a transparent river.

#9

垂柳疏疏綠又新	The weeping willows sparsely set are green and new again;
經霜了不染微塵	Though facing the frost they are not ever tainted by dust.
索居難出淩霄塔	Living in isolation you rarely find a sky-high tower;
願作榆城一畫人	I'd rather stay just a painter in the Elm City.[43]

---

38. There is a common proverb stating that blue dye comes from the indigo plant but is even bluer.
39. "Lone wandering" is a common expression for the thinkers and writers of the Wei-Jin era.
40. "Flying white" means painting or writing with a dry brush.
41. This line adapts one of Li Shangyin's "Untitled" poems. See Liu, *The Poetry of Li Shang-yin*, 66.
42. The blurry style of Mi Fu 米芾 (1051–1107) and his son Mi Youren 米友仁 (1074–1153).
43. The Elm City is New Haven, CT.

#10

遠浦低昂日欲斜	On a distant shore, rising and falling, the sunlight falls aslant;
寒鴉數點即天涯	A few specks there of winter crows, at the edge of the sky.
孤舟一繫心千里	Like a lone boat my heart is tethered miles away.[44]
且傍蘆花處處家	Here alongside the flowering reeds the houses stand.

#11

婀娜柔條可待秋	How can they abide the autumn, these soft branches lithely swaying?
孤亭寒水去悠悠	I leave far behind a lonely pavilion on a frozen river.
廿年我亦天南客	These twenty years I too am a traveler south of Heaven.
不為看山始白頭	It was not because of these mountains that my hair first whitened.

#12

排闥兩山入眼青	Opening the door, two mountains come greenly into view;[45]
疏林長阪舊曾經	The sparse forest and the tall hills are ones I passed before.
回頭三十年前事	Looking back over the events of these thirty years behind,
猶有泉聲護草亭	A stream still burbles here beside the grassy pavilions.

#13

派衍隔山出愈奇	Different channels set apart by mountains produce greater and greater marvels;
平沙折葦雁來時	Level sands and reeds aslant, the geese are now coming back.
筆端芍藥偏含雨	The tip of my brush is a peony still wet with rain;
肘外寒蟬獨掛枝	Beyond my elbows the winter cicada hangs from a branch alone.

#14

忍寒艸樹更含滋	After enduring much cold, the grasses and trees grow even lusher;
岸赭山青又一奇	The banks of ochre and emerald hills offer yet another wonder.
隔磵苔深岩骨峭	Across the ravine the moss is deep, bonelike crags protruding;
冷泉流夢忽移時	Chill streams flow by like dreams, passing in an instant.

---

44. See Du Fu's "Autumn Meditations" #8, *Du shi xiangzhu* 17.1497.

45. Adapting a line by Wang Anshi 王安石 (1021–1086): "Two mountains, like opening the door, send in their green." See *Wang Jingwen gong shi jianzhu* 43.574.

#15

屋外平添湖水深	Beyond the buildings level extend the lake waters in their depths;
湖風吹雨綠成陰	The breeze on the lake scatters raindrops into the green shade.[46]
也知鶴唳渾如昔	I still know the cry of the crane that goes unchanged.
愁聽昏鴉更滿林	How melancholy to hear the evening crows as they occupy the forest.

#16

搖落江山萬里遙	Rivers and mountains rise and fall ten thousand leagues into the distance;
何人此處泛蘭橈	Who is that man there floating along on orchid-scented oars?
斷崖空自懸千尺	The sheer cliffs hang down a thousand feet into nothingness;
隔水林風我欲招	Across these waters through the forest breeze I'll call out to him.[47]

---

46. Here 蔭 is emended to 陰 to fit the rhyme.
47. This quatrain was inscribed on a landscape painting by Jao's contemporary Van I-pong 萬一鵬 (1917–1994).

Inscribed on My Own Landscape Paintings[48]

These quatrains recall the seventeenth-century painter Zhang Feng 張風, a.k.a. Zhang Dafeng 張大風. Dafeng literally means "great wind."

#1

登高誰解說山川	Even by climbing up high how can you explain a landscape?
老樹魁梧已百年	The aged trees have stood formidably a century already.
商略雲端今四皓	Chatting above the clouds, the Four Hoaryheads of today;[49]
人間回首幾桑田	How many times past have mulberry groves been transformed?[50]

#2

古苔和墨翠如簪	The ancient moss suits my ink, halcyon as a hatpin.[51]
亂石橫空鎖碧灘	Random stones crossing the void fill an azure pool.[52]
入夢大風吹垢去	Entering a dream, a great wind came to blow the filth away.
樹猶如此人何堪	If even trees are thus, how can any man bear it?[53]

---

48. 自題山水. *Wenji* 563. Jao's note: When this painting was finished, someone said the style was similar to that of Zhang Dafeng. [For more on Zhang and his background, see Jao's article "Zhang Dafeng ji qi jiashi" 張大風及其家世, *Rao Zongyi ershi shiji xueshu wenji* 18: 488–519.] I recalled how in the annals of Emperors and Kings, the Yellow Emperor dreamed of a great wind blowing through the whole realm, sweeping away all the dust and grime. The Emperor awoke and lamented: "This wind has performed my command!" Then he obtained his minister, the Master of Winds, at the edge of the ocean. Zhang Feng took this phrase as his *nom de plume*, perhaps with such a subtle meaning in mind. Thus I have written about the propitious quality of the "great wind," which reminds us of the dream of the Yellow Emperor. Composed by Hsüan-t'ang ten days before the Winter Solstice of 1976.

49. The Four Hoaryheads were four recluses from around the time of the fall of the Han dynasty.

50. I.e., transformed into oceans; a common figure for the transformations effected by the passage of time.

51. "Halcyon" means greenish-blue like kingfisher feathers; the "hatpin" a metal ornament used in the hair of imperial officials.

52. Here 澤 is emended to 灘 to fit the rhyme.

53. Huan Wen made this remark when he saw that willows he had planted had already grown to a circumference of ten spans. See *Shishuo xinyu* 2/55.

Inscribed on a Painting of Orchids by Ma Shouzhen: Variation on a Line of Rongfu's[54]

Ma Xianglan 馬湘蘭 (1548–1604), a.k.a. Ma Shouzhen, was a poet and painter particularly celebrated for her paintings of orchids. Rongfu refers to the writer Wang Zhong 汪中 (1745–1794).

夕韭朝菘看滿田	See how evening leeks and morning cabbages fill the fields.
寒流清泚送華年	Cool streams sparkle as they pass along the blossoming years.
靈思已使叢蘭泣	Some spiritual longing has already made the orchids weep.
宿恨徒教子墨鐫	A long-borne and futile regret causes Sir Ink to chisel out writings.[55]
掩抑荒烟芳艸陌	Downcast in desolate mists, fragrant grasses on the paths,
支離疏柳夕陽天	A few sparsely standing willows and a sunset-red sky.
浮生相感空啼哭	Touched by something in this floating life and crying without reason,
訴與哀絃祇惘然	I make my plaint on sorrowful strings telling of my hopelessness.

---

54. 題馬守真蘭卷，檃括容甫句為詩. *Wenji* 506.
55. Sir Ink is a character in Yang Xiong's "Rhapsody on the Tall Poplars Palace." See Knechtges, *Wen xuan*, 2:139.

Essay on Cloudgazing[56]

I completed my painting of *Cloudgazing*, but did not have time to compose an inscription. After being reprimanded by Pan Xuzhi,[57] I have supplemented an inscription on new paper. The cranes were not isolated but I added a duck; the flowers were displaced but I have connected them with trees. But my poetic inspiration was long blocked, and I could not fulfill Xuzhi's request. Then I looked at Chen Yuyi's *Essay on Juexin's Painting of Mountains and Rivers*, and all at once achieved a new insight into it.[58] So I composed a *fu* according to his rhymes, as follows:

以畫代簡	One can use painting to substitute for a letter,
以夢通禪	Use dreams to enter into meditation.
山增憒憒	Mountains inspire a vague and misty feeling,
水極人天	Rivers join together men and Heaven.
5 誰付無文之印	Whoever could carve a wordless seal
且屬常臞之仙	Would stay an immortal ever slender and youthful.
意開遮以自在	Clouds open and close spontaneously as they please,
氣恍惚而出山	Aimlessly departing the hills in a burst of air.
方飛揚乎六合	Just as they soar out beyond the six directions,
10 忽收斂于半間	All at once they collect back into half a space.[59]

山南山北	South of the mountains and north of the mountains,
乍吐乍吞	Here they breathe out and there they swallow up.
升如蒸餾	They rise like steam,
出似軍屯	Depart in military formation.
15 蔽虧戶牖	They block and occlude the doors and windows,
被覆岡巒	Cover and conceal the hills and ridges.
排之不易	It is not easy to displace them,
攬之良難	Harder still to seize them in the hand.
以道觀之	Observing them according to the Way,
20 於意自安	The clouds grow still of their own will.

---

56. 觀雲賦. *Wenji* 278.

57. Pan Shou 潘受 (1911–1999), distinguished Singaporean calligrapher and classical poet, was a native of Fujian province.

58. Chen Yuyi 陳與義 (1090–1138) was a Song dynasty poet.

59. Bei Qiong 貝瓊 (d. 1379) wrote a "Record of Clouds in Half a Space" 半間雲記. See *Qingjiang Bei xiansheng ji* 10.3a–4a.

亙萬古而無所住	Through the ten thousand ages they have not stayed in any place,
顧嘗未交乎一言	Never have they been seen to exchange a single word.
初默然於朝澈	At first in silence they disperse with the morning,
視飛鳥之破煙	Watching the birds fly past through the mist.
25 譬犯雪山	They might be likened to trespassing on a snowy mountain,
如巢絕壁	Or be compared to birds nesting in a sheer wall,
野馬絪縕	Or to wild horses shifting shape,
周旋四側	Turning over this way and that.
叩帝閽之浩浩	They knock at God's threshold in its vastness,
30 去人寰之嘖嘖	Depart the thundering chatter of the human realm.
接前境之非真	They develop out of the manifest realm's unreality,
悟來者之皆實	And perceive all the substance in future beings.
說法由假	Talk of the dharma derives from what is false,
忘言惟臆	Forgetting words depends on one's own will.
35 看表裏之山河	Looking over the face and the reverse of the mountains and rivers,
豈頃刻所嘗歷	How is it something traversable in a moment?
謂雲之為吾耶	Do you say that the clouds are myself?
則隨合前開	But as they join together and open up,
來往而靡一相識	They go and come without anything I recognize.
40 謂吾之非雲耶	Do you say that I am not the clouds?
則何故迷離惝恍	Then why am I so confused and astray,
留此似是而非之跡	Leaving behind these apparently real but false traces?
虛之聞而不言	Xuzhi heard but did not speak,
頷其持之有故	Just nodded in sure assent.
45 隔千里兮一笑	With a laugh one thousand miles away,
袖浮雲兮夢中以去	Folding the floating clouds into a sleeve of dream, he departed.

To the Tune of "Recalling the Sound of Panpipes on the Phoenix Terrace": On the Withering of the Azalea[60]

This lyric is not literally about painting, but the imagery throughout is so visually rich that it is the verbal equivalent of one. In Chinese the name for "azalea" (dujuanhua) is the same as the cuckoo. Its red blossoms represent the tears of blood wept out by the ancient prince Du Yu, whose soul was transformed into a cuckoo.

雨急還收	The rain is abrupt and then pauses;
雲開仍閉	the clouds break and close again,
春陰只在高樓	spring shadows left only in high towers.
望星星鴻沒	I watch the great geese vanish like stars,
夢渺神州	and dream of the Continent of Spirits far off.[61]
休譜湘南怨曲	Don't write those bitter tunes of Southern Xiang,
怕風起落葉成秋	I fear the passing wind will cause the leaves to fall, creating autumn.
清明近	The tomb-sweeping festival is near,[62]
夕陽芳草	the fragrant grasses in the evening sun
一樣風流	have a romance of their own.

* * *

江頭	At the riverhead
新蒲細柳	are young rushes and lithe willows;
傍水面殘花	By the water facing the surviving blossoms,
淚點難收	these teardrops are hard to gather up,
況杜鵑血泣	Let alone the azalea weeping blood,
紅上簾鉤	blushing up over the curtain hooks.
波外美人何處	Where beyond the waves has that fair lady gone?
黯關山	Dimly I gaze on the mountain passes,
千里凝眸[63]	focusing pupils over these thousand leagues:
清鐘動	A pure bell resounds,
曾濤孤嶠	like layered waves on lonely peaks,
落雁遙舟	a far-off boat amid descending geese—

---

60. 鳳凰臺上憶吹簫・杜鵑謝後有寄. *Wenji* 570.
61. A traditional term for China with Daoist resonance.
62. The tomb-sweeping festival (Qingming 清明) occurs at the beginning of April each year.
63. Here 眸 is emended to 眸 to fit rhyme.

To the Tune of "Spring Comes from Heaven Above": For Painting Master Tang Yun[64]

At that time Tang had just come from Wumen in Fujian province and was living by Diamond Hill in Kowloon.

白社凋零	The white shrine is desolate now;[65]
認劫後河山	I recognize the rivers and hills after the catastrophe
草上微螢	like faint fireflies upon the grass.
溪漾流月	The moon floats by upon the creek,
影墜羅屏	its shadow falling on a gauze screen.
心逐去雁冥冥	My heart follows the departing geese into the void.
任無風花嚲	Let there be no wind and flowers dangling behind;
問知己	I ask my friend who understands
剩有山靈	if the mountain spirit is still there.
短長聲	The voice may be short or long,
更啼紅杜宇	As the crimson cuckoo calls out again,
啄翠清泠	pecking at the halcyon trees in their pure remoteness—

* * *

當前雲煙畫本	Just before me a sketchbook of clouds and mist,
伴隱几噓天	leaning over my desk I sigh before Heaven,
冷落晨星	where the morning stars are few and solitary.
縱目關河	Letting my gaze roam upon passes and rivers,
鑄愁今古	I'll cast in bronze the sorrows of past and present,
鄉夢祇挂門庭	and hang my dream of home upon the gateway.
便琴書拋了	Thus my zither and books discarded,
人憔悴	myself frail and weak,
未負丹青	I have not yet betrayed the green and red of painting.
醉還醒	When I've sobered up,
只暗蛩寒蚓	Only the locusts of the night and winter worms
來共青熒	come to share the flickering candlelight.

---

64. 春從天上來・贈畫師唐雲. *Wenji* 570. Following the rhymes of Wu Yan'gao 吳彥高.

65. "White shrine" denotes the residence of a recluse. It originally referred to a specific site near Luoyang.

To the Tune of "Lips Dotted with Rouge": Inscribed on Tang Yun's Painting of Flight to Yaoshan[66]

Another poem inspired by Tang's painting.

刺眼奇峰	Glancing at the strange peaks
當年曾是經行處	and places I stopped some other year,
朔風如虎	The North Wind is like a tiger
山上斜陽舞	while oblique rays of evening sun shimmer on the hills.

* * *

又向天涯	I turn again toward the edge of Heaven
蓬轉驚如故	where the tumbleweed turns as rapidly as ever.
心無住	My heart has no place to remain,
漫勞縑素	So I'll trouble this canvas of plain taffeta,
覓取歸時路	Searching for a road to return.

---

66. 點絳唇・唐雲為作瑤山行役圖,因題其上. *Wenji* 578.

To the Tune of "Bodhisattva Barbarian"[67]

The painting technique mentioned in the first line is simple, yet highly suggestive of Jao's particular vision of the world.

人生到處如敷采	Everywhere in this life is like colors washed over ink,
苕華謝去春仍在	Though the trumpet blossoms have withered the spring remains.
流水自朝朝	The rivers flow on day after day,
關心上下潮	I'll watch the rising and receding tides.

* * *

清愁和淚煮	My pure sorrows boil along with tears,
欲共蘭成語	I want to share a conversation with Lancheng.[68]
午夢試重溫	I'll try to revive a dream of noonday,
黃鸝又叩門	When the yellow oriole knocks at the door again.

---

67. 菩薩蠻. *Wenji* 580. Man 蠻 is really a specific southern people neighboring the Han, but euphony demands "Bodhisattva Barbarian."

68. The "*Fu* on Sorrow" 愁賦 is attributed to Yu Xin 庾信 (513–581). Only eight lines survive, including: "With what can you boil sorrow until it is cooked through?" See *Yu Zishan jizhu* 1094 (appendix). Lancheng was one of Yu Xin's style names.

To the Tune of "Charms of Niannu": For a Collection of My Calligraphy and Painting[69]

Shen Meisou (1849–1923) said: "Once you have passed through the barrier of Yuanjia's landscape,[70] then the 'moon of detachment' appears spontaneously there." The "moon of detachment" is a phrase from the Huayan Sutra, and I borrow its meaning here.[71]

萬峰如睡	The myriad peaks seem to sleep:
看人世污染	looking upon the pollution of the human world,
竟成何物	what has it all become?
幸有靈犀相照徹	Fortunately illuminated by numinous rhinoceros horn,
靜對圖書滿壁	In silence I face a shelf full of books.
石不能言	Stones cannot speak,
花非解語	nor flowers parse our speech,
惆悵東欄雪	grieving in the snow on the East Veranda.
江山呈秀	While rivers and mountains show off their blooms,
待論書海英傑	let's chat instead about masters from the ocean of texts.

* * *

細說畫裡陽秋	Closely reading the Spring and Autumn Annals in the painting,[72]
心源了悟	an insight into the sources of the heart
興自清秋發	rises out of this clear autumn.
想象荒煙榛莽處	Imagine that wild place of mists within the underbrush,
妙筆飛鴻明滅	where the soaring goose of a subtle brush appears and then vanishes.

---

69. 念奴嬌・自題書畫集. *Wenji* 753; *Ershi shiji shi da jia ci xuan* 309.
70. Yuanjia 元嘉 was the style name of Wan Zuoheng 萬祚亨, a late-Ming landscape painter.
71. Specifically, it is the name of a Buddha. See *T* 293:10.801c.
72. See *Shishuo xinyu* 8/66, which uses the similar phrase "Spring and Autumn Annals in a human skin" 皮裡陽秋, referring to someone who makes clear judgments in his mind without enunciating them. Cf. Mather, *Shih-shuo hsin-yü*, 245.

騎省縱橫	That Departmental Cavalier [Xu Xuan] wrote unrestrainedly;[73]
文通破墨	the Master of Writing [Zhang Zao] painted in diluted ink.[74]
冥契通窮髮	Through this secret concord of minds we can reach far as the Hairless Pole.[75]
好山好水	Fine mountains, fine rivers:
胸中解脫寒月	I find in my own breast detachment like the winter moon!

---

73. Jao's note: Zhu Xi 朱熹 (1130–1200) commented on the calligraphy of Xu Xuan 徐鉉 (916–991), "He roams unrestrained and wild, without even the slightest show or pose." Wang Shizhen (1526–1590), however, said: "When he copied the Yi Mountain Stele, he only matched the forms. When you look for the special charm of the scattered traces of snowdrift, the wild geese fluttering together, you find yourself imagining only the overgrown brush in the wild mists, and so must heave another sigh." The great Xu himself said that he had "obtained his master somewhere between Heaven and Man." I would not dare to compare myself with Master Xu, but merely thought of these words, and tried to express my own thoughts on it.

74. Zhang Zao 張璪, the Tang painter whose "diluted ink" technique (using water to dilute ink into various shades which then combine for a rich, multilayered effect) is mentioned, along with Wang Wei's, in Zhang Yanyuan, *Lidai minghua ji*, 10.318.

75. The Hairless Pole is the northern extremity too cold for any living thing to survive.

To the Tune of "Music for Welcoming Spring": On a Polychrome Brick Mural of Human Figures in the Collection of the Boston Museum of Fine Arts[76]

The charming murals preserved in Han dynasty tombs might serve as a fitting subject for any poet, but Jao's signature is in the final line: an allusion to yet another Han-era painting attested only in the textual tradition. The whole poem laments how much of China's cultural heritage has been lost, while celebrating the beauty of those traces that remain.

誰家燕子辭華屋	Swallows leave the gorgeous eaves of someone's home:
銜泥去	Bearing mud to build nests,
度簾熟	they measure the screen closely.
念古悲有限駒光速	I find that ancient sorrows do end once time's stallion races past:
苔上蝕	Dissolving under moss,
城狐宿	while foxes nest in the walls.

*   *   *

人物斑斕磚一束	Human figures speckling a bundle of bricks;
舊曾是瘞紅銷綠	This was where the reds were buried and the greens destroyed.
見說北風圖	I have heard of the "Portrait of the North Wind,"
思蜀繪	recall those canvases of Shu
悲寒玉	and grieve for winter jade.[77]

---

76. 迎春樂・題漢墓磚人物彩繪，波士頓美術館藏. *Wenji* 632.

77. Jao's note: Gu Kaizhi's 顧愷之 (341–402) essay "On Painting" says that the "Poem and Painting of the North Wind" was by Wei Xie. It was not unlike that by Liu Bao 劉褒 (147–167) of Yizhou [in the ancient kingdom of Shu, modern Sichuan].

VIII

The Sound of the Qin

Jao is an accomplished player of the qin 琴 (the seven-stringed board instrument sometimes translated as "zither"), as well as being a collector of the instrument. Musical, artistic, and literary expression are not separate fields for Jao, but instead are mutually inspiring and sustaining. In the preface to his "Cheung Chau Collection" he comments:[1]

> In the ten years since I moved to the south [to Hong Kong], for a long period I stopped composing my own verses. Since I learned to play on the silk strings, though, I began to compose a bit again. Is this because the spirit of poetry and the spirit of the *qin* may support and complement one another?

Jao means primarily shi *poetry here and suggests that the kind of inchoate melancholy and nostalgia so perfectly expressed in* qin *melodies also motivates his composition of these poems. But he depicts both the performance and enjoyment of* qin *music most explicitly in his* ci *lyrics, and indeed there is a special affinity between music and the expressive mode of* ci*, which tend to be organized around loose association of imagery rather than strictly logical sequences.*

---

1. *Wenji* 462.

Illustration 9. *Playing the Qin* (1970s).

To the Tune of "Eight Voices in Ganzhou"[2]

I brought my zither to the ocean on an autumn evening. The multitudinous sounds of the universe fell silent, and in the pure echoes faintly overheard I felt lost in another epoch altogether.

共水天入定	Entering meditation alongside water and sky,
渺蒼煙	that azure haze in the distance:
山色有無中	"the aspect of mountains between being there and not."[3]
忽泠泠霜響	All at once a frosty echo heard faintly,
濺濺石瀨	like rivulets burbling through rocks,
遙答鳴蟲	distantly answers the chirping crickets.
不耐琴心挑引	My qin-like mind couldn't help but be teased,
冷月尚惺忪	as the cold moon still perfectly aware of everything;
但聽商聲起	But I heard the note of the autumn sounding,
處處秋風	and gales blew all around.

* * *

猶有徵招遺韻	An echo of the tune "Summoned" lingers here[4]
似孤飛野鶴	resembling a wild crane that flies alone
去住無蹤	coming and going without a trace.[5]
望愁漪千頃	I gaze at ripples of sorrow a thousand yards wide:
隔海意難通	a feeling that cannot traverse the ocean.
寫吳絲	Reflected in a zither of Wu silk,
凝雲流水	dense clouds and flowing water,
恐馮夷	I fear the River God
深夜出幽宮	will leave his Palace of Darkness tonight.
沉吟久	Though I chant on alone
成連何在	where is there a Chenglian to teach me
海氣濛濛	of the ocean and air in all their vastness?[6]

---

2. 八聲甘州. *Wenji* 571.
3. This line is a direct quotation from Wang Wei's poem "Sailing Down the Han River" 漢江臨汎 (*Quan Tang shi* 126.1279).
4. *Ci* tune created by Jiang Kui.
5. These lines are based on a description of Jiang Kui's style by Zhang Yan 張炎: "Like wild clouds in solitary flight, staying and departing without a trace." See *Ci yuan* B.6a.
6. Chenglian was a famous musician from the Spring and Autumn period, the teacher of Boya.

To the Tune of "Evening Moon in Spring on the Xiang River"[7]

This ci *lyric is inspired by the* qin *melody "Xiao and Xiang Rivers." The poet revels in the interrelated images of memory, music, and feeling that the melody evokes.*

漾空明	Floating over the moonlit waves,
柳風偏攪離魂	the breeze from the willows seems to stir my solitary soul.
可奈別館憎憎	How hard to bear the stillness in the guest lodge,
千念集晨昏	a thousand thoughts gathering at dawn and dusk.
試欲折花歸去	I'd like to cull some blossoms and return with them,
恐簪花人老	unless that beauty with flower hairpin has grown old now,
不當芳春	and cannot bear the fragrant spring.
但野煙恨水	There is only an uninhabited mist and a river of resentment,
清冷萬里	a serene chill that extends one thousand miles,
情往思存	where love is lost but longing stays.

                *   *   *

滄桑一角	Oceans have turned into mulberry groves there:[8]
悲生極浦	grief comes to the farthest shore,
垂涕雍門	and I shed tears for Yongmen.[9]
獨撫危絃	I pluck the lofty string alone,
還髣髴	and it almost seems
滿湖青草	as if the lake and its green grasses are
寒浸湘雲	steeped in the chill of Xiang clouds.
江南夢遠	The dream of the Southland is far off,
怕此時	and I fear this moment
都種愁根	will plant another seed of sorrow.
剩伴我	The only companions I have now
有飛鳶點點	are the kites that flit here and there,
蘆邊雁影	the geese's shadows against the reeds,
天上星痕	traces of stars in the sky.

---

    7. 湘春夜月. *Wenji* 586–587. Jao's preface: I enjoy playing the qin melody "Xiao and Xiang," which reminds me of White Stone's lines "The clouds of Xiang and the waters of Chu are stirred, / Gazing into the distance wounds my heart" 蕩湘雲楚水，目極傷心, and the note of repressed feeling there. I elaborated on these lines, following the rhymes of Xuezhou [Huang Xiaomai 黃孝邁].
    8. A common figure for the rapid transformations of human life.
    9. Yongmen Zizhou 雍門子周 was a master qin player whose performance made his listener weep. See *Shuo yuan jiaozheng* 11.279.

To the Tune of "Severe Cold Syncopation"[10]

This piece is dedicated to an ancient qin, described as early as a thirteenth-century manual, and now owned by Jao himself.

冰絃漫譜衡陽雁	On icy strings plucking out the tune of "Hengyang Geese,"[11]
西風野日蕭索	desolate as the west wind under a bleak sun.
草衰塞外	The grasses have withered beyond the pass,
霜飛隴上	frost gathering upon the hills,
兩三邊角	while two or three border horns sound.[12]
江波又惡	The waves on the river are wild again:
況憔悴征衫漸薄	my traveling robe hangs loose on my emaciated body.
似聲聲	It seems as if every voice
黃雲莽莽	is the yellow clouds drifting in the vastness of space,
嘶馬度沙漠	the whinnying horses crossing the desert.

                        *   *   *

遙想京城裏	I imagine the sound inside a faraway palace,
裂帛當歌	high voices like shredded silks,
索鈴行樂	playing a song with "looped chimes."[13]
雲煙過眼	As clouds and mist pass before my eyes
算而今	I reckon that now
軫催髹落	the frets are worn and the lacquer chipped away.

---

    10. 凄涼犯. *Wenji* 583. Jao's preface: Zhou Mi's (1232–1298) *Record of Things Seen and Heard at Infinity Studio* contains an item on a famous qin from the North. Guo Tianxi (1227–1302) from Jincheng had given him an instrument called "Ten Thousand Valley Pine." Xianyu Shu's (1246–1302) *Miscellaneous Register from the Studio of Hard Learning*, under the section on famous qins from the capital, also mentions a "Ten Thousand Valley Pine" zither recently made by Guo Beishan. This qin now belongs to me. I obtained it from Mr. Gu, after Zou Jingquan had brought it to Guangdong province from the north. Each time I play the "Ditty from an Autumn Pass" on a frosty morning, I am overcome by a sense of loss and desolation. I have followed the inspiration of the White-Stone Daoist, writing to the tune of his "Auspicious Cranes and Reflections of Immortals" [an alternate name for this tune].

    11. There is a peak on Mount Heng near Hengyang (in Hunan province), past which it was said that geese were not willing to travel. A qin tune "Geese Passing Hengyang" 雁渡衡陽 refers to this legend.

    12. Jao cites a couplet by Bai Juyi: "Border horns with two or three branches, / Under frosty skies young men on the hillocks." See *Bai Juyi ji* 25.555.

    13. Jao's note: A method of playing the qin.

漫有知音	At last there is one who knows the tune,
隔千載	across one thousand years
重為護著	another protector for you.
寄悲哀	I pass on to you this sorrow and this grief:
萬壑競響許夢約	the myriad ravines resounding together to requite the promise of a dream.[14]

---

14. Jao's note: As in the original line, I have used seven deflected tones here. [Translator's note: Chinese prosody relies on an artful balance of "level" and "deflected" tones in each line. Seven in a row is extremely unusual and gives to this line a ringing fortissimo. Jao's note also mentions that two lines in Jiang's original poem do not fit the rhyme, and that he has not preserved this feature in his poem.]

To the Tune of "Prelude to a Water Melody"[15]

Another piece dedicated to the same qin, *one of Jao's prized possessions.*

此曲幾人解	How many understand this tune?
搔首叩旻天	Scratching my head I address Bright Heaven.
女媧何故多變	Why is Nü Wa so changeable?
搏土自何年	When was it that she molded clay?[16]
不學敲鐘鳴鼓	I do not know how to strike the bell or beat the drum,
但以冰絃　拂	only how to play along the icy strings
指上弄清寒	and strum the pure chill with my fingertips.
嫋嫋繞梁去	The music delicately circles the purlins overhead
餘響落花間	and echoes amid the blossoms fallen below.

* * *

起山鬼	Spirits rise in the mountains,
隱霧豹	leopards hide in the fog;
驚愁眠	I too am startled from sorrow's slumber.
別無長物	Nothing else is permanent
窺戶剛見月纔圓	but the moon growing full in the windowpane.
欲起湘靈鼓瑟	I want to raise the Spirit of the Xiang River to pluck the zither.[17]
休作商聲變徵	Don't play anymore those notes of Shang or deviant Zhi;[18]
意怯理能全	though the mind is weak the pattern can still be made whole.
待乘埃風去	Let's ride together on the dusty breeze,
換骨託嬋娟	exchange these earthly bones for moonlit beauty.

---

15. 水調歌頭. 654–655. *Ershi shiji shi da jia ci xuan* 305–306. Jao's preface: About to return east, my books and possessions all packed away, I had on my person only my qin, the "ten thousand valley pine." Sleepless in the middle of the night, I woke up and played a song to pass the time and express my feelings to Heaven. Since I sailed my raft to the Southern Ocean, I have been rushing hither and thither for two decades. Now, the bright moonlight entering my bosom, surveying present and past, I composed this poem to the rhymes of old East Slope.

16. Goddess Nü Wa is said to have fashioned human beings out of clay.

17. Jao's note: This refers to Louis Chen, a classical musician who often played together with me.

18. Shang and deviant Zhi are two of the seven notes of the classical scale, both associated with melancholy tunes.

IX

On Poetry

This section presents some of the poems in which Jao suggests his own theory of poetic composition. The prefaces to his poetry collections tend to provide modest disclaimers of any serious intent, so it is within the poems themselves we must look for any general views. One of the most striking themes is his emphasis on the ineffable quality of artistic inspiration, a conception strongly influenced by Jao's knowledge of Buddhism.

Cheung Chau Collection #18[1]

This poem is a sort of Ars Poetica embellished by variations on the descriptive and symbolic significance of the word "flower," a practical exemplification of the theory that is summed up in the reverberations of the Buddhist term "heart-flowers."[2]

去日盡如夢	Past days are gone like a dream,
夢中意獨傾	A dream toward which my mind still inclines.
綺語偶一為	Occasionally I'll weave satin sentences,
聊以破沉冥	To dissolve encroaching dark a while.
嫣然心花開	Heart-flowers bloom in lyrical loveliness;
簾罅吐春榮	Through a chink in the curtains burst spring colors.
此心如朝徹	Should this one heart find "morning insight,"
種種今日生	Then "pure simplicity" might begin today.[3]
吟白幾莖髭	Chanting will whiten a few strands of mustache,[4]
坐對青燈熒	We sit before the green lamps' glow.
燈花與盆花	Lamps' waxen blossoms and a flowerpot
粲比二難並	Seem magnificent as the "two unobtainable things."[5]
甘苦敢喻人	Not daring tell a soul of my joys and my suffering,
但取慰吾情	I take only enough to console my own heart.

---

1. *Wenji* 467.
2. "Heart-flowers" occurs, for instance, in the Huayan sutra (*T* 278: 9.616b).
3. This couplet combines two allusions to *Zhuangzi*, the first describing the highest state of awareness and enlightenment, the second a term of praise for the commonfolk. See *Zhuangzi* 6.252 and 10.359, respectively.
4. The same idea that poetic composition whitens one's mustache occurs in "Presented to Yu Fu" 贈喻鳧 by Fang Gan 方干 (809–888) (see *Quan Tang shi* 648.7444).
5. The "two unobtainable things" are "to know the springs of action" and "though being distant in friendship—yet still to be sincere in what one says." See *Shishuo xinyu* 10/6; Mather, *A New Account of Tales of the World*, 297–298. Cf. Wang Bo's "Preface for Parting at the Pavilion of Prince Teng in Denghongfu on an Autumn Day" 秋日登洪府滕王閣餞別序, *Wang Zi'an jizhu* 8.232.

Cheung Chau Collection #62[6]

The final couplet refers to a common Buddhist saying, to the effect that a blind person has the capacity to imagine seeing beautiful flowers, but if his sight were restored he would no longer be able to see them at all.

高山即高士	Lofty mountains are like lofty gentlemen:
自為天外賓	They seem to be visitors from beyond the heavens.
搔背有麻姑	When you scratch your back with Auntie Hemp's talons;[7]
幾見海揚塵	You almost begin to see dust rising upon the ocean.
我詩不自惜	I do not prize these poems myself;
出句若有神	The verses appear as if a spirit had bestowed them.
如植空中花	Poetry is like planting flowers in the air;
奈何多翳人	But how else to help a man whose has lost his sight?

---

6. *Wenji* 477.

7. Auntie Hemp was a Daoist immortal with birdlike talons, which a foolish mortal man wanted to use to scratch his back. See *Taiping guangji* 60.370.

Cheung Chau Collection #82[8]

Poetry is seen here as an embodiment of unity between the individual and the cosmos, and also simultaneously as a discipline of self-perfection.

詩無乎不在	There is nowhere that poetry is not present.
瓦甓亦賁華	Even the tiles and bricks are embellished with flowers.
豈不思古人	I cannot help but think of the ancients:
易奇而詩葩	Of the *Changes* rare and strange, and the blossoming *Odes*.
老驥千里心	An aged stallion with its mind set on a thousand leagues
猶秣天山禾	Can still feed on the millet of Heaven Mountain.[9]
誰能寫其真	Who can describe the reality of things,
而求世俗阿	While also seeking the flattery of the vulgar?
真氣果吐虹	My vital spirit perfected, I can breathe out rainbows:
覽者莫驚嗟	Dear reader, please do not be startled!

---

8. *Wenji* 482.

9. Heaven Mountain (Tianshan), located in modern Xinjiang province, represents the distant frontier. The couplet reverses Su Shi's "How pitiful that aged stallion, now truly aged! / Without any longer the will to feed on the millet of Heaven Mountain." See *Su Shi shiji* 25.1352.

To the Tune of "Butterflies Admiring Blossoms": Playfully Composed on an Offering of Paper Flowers[10]

This poem at first appears to be a light pastiche of an ancient tradition of ci *lyrics on flowers. But its simplicity is entirely deceptive, as its ten lines interweave a series of dichotomies—nature and art, truth and falsity, life and poetry, seriousness and frivolity—so that none remains as simple as at first sight.*

人間無復埋花處	No longer any place to bury flowers in the mortal realm;
為怕花殘	Because we fear the flowers might be hurt:
莫買真花去	please don't buy any real flowers!
靜對瓊枝相爾汝	In silence facing jadelike branches we speak in familiar names,[11]
膽瓶覷面成賓主	In the gall-shaped vase I see your face and we become host and guest.

* * *

詞客生生花裏住	For the writer of lyrics a lifetime is lived amid the flowers:
剪裁冰綃	Trimming and chopping to make ice-like chiffon,
留寫傷春句	composing verses to mourn the spring.
紫蝶黃蜂渾不與	Purple butterflies and honeybees won't consort with them.[12]
任他日日閒風雨	They are left to spend their days in the wind and rain.

---

10. 蝶戀花：以紙花清供戲賦. *Wenji* 569; *Ershi shiji shi da jia ci xuan* 276–278.
11. Cf. Han Yu 韓愈 (768–824), "Listening to Master Ying Play the Qin" 聽穎師彈琴: "Intimate the words of boys and girls, / In gratitude and resentment using familiar names [*se tutoyant*]" (*Quan Tang shi* 340.3813).
12. See Li Shangyin, "The Second Day of the Second Month" 二月二日, "Flower pistils and willowy eyes each cannot be relied on, / Purple butterflies and honeybees all have passions of their own" (cf. Liu, *The Poetry of Li Shang-yin*, 162).

To the Tune of "Bodhisattva Barbarian": Crooked Cap Songs[13]

This poem is a celebration of the Manchu lyricist Nalan Xingde 納蘭性德 (1655–1685). Jao's preface cites Wang Guowei's citation of Nietzsche's maxim "Schreibe mit Blut!" [Write with blood], evoking the passionate intensity of Nalan's work.

人間冰雪為誰熱	Who will melt the ice and snow in human hearts?
新詞恰似啼鵑血	New lyrics are just like the blood of a cuckoo in song,[14]
血也不成書	Though the blood does not write an entire book.
眼枯淚欲無	When the eyes are dried the tears are nearly gone.

* * *

風鬟連雨鬢	Hair curled like the breeze, temples like rain:
偏是來無準	But I cannot tell when she will come.
吹夢到如今	Blow that dream further on into the present,
有情海樣深	For my passion is profound as the sea.

---

13. 菩薩蠻・題側帽詞. *Wenji* 581. *Crooked Cap Songs* is the title of one of Nalan Xingde's collections of *ci*.

14. The cuckoo represents the spirit of the wronged soul Du Yu, ancient King of Shu. After losing his kingdom and perishing, his soul was transformed into a cuckoo, which kept singing until it cried in blood.

To the Tune of "Whole River Red": On Reading the Poetry of Li He[15]

Jao combines allusions to Li He's poetry in an evocation of human frailty.

日上三竿	The sun has risen three bamboo poles high,
休報道先生睡足	but please do not report that the master has slept enough.
偶墜向	I sometimes face
文章劫裡	a curse that forces me to write
碧緗盈束	till my emerald books form a bundle.
年少空教簫化淚	In youth you waste time turning flute music into tears;
蹉跎早是髀生肉	strolling along soon will put fat on your thighs.[16]
但徘徊	But when you dally here
眸子射酸風	your pupils are struck by acid gales
看新局	as you look on the fresh scene.[17]

* * *

蘭欲笑	The orchids will smile,
雞可卜	the chickens can be used for divination.[18]
琴已瘦	The zithers are already emaciated,
腸仍曲	our innards still wrenched.[19]
遍人間	All over the human realm
坐閱山丘華屋	I see mansions reverting to mounds of earth.

---

15. 滿江紅・讀昌谷詩. *Wenji* 614.

16. Liu Bei once lamented that while he was waiting in Jingzhou and no longer in the saddle of a campaign, his thighs were growing fat and old age was advancing. See *San guo zhi* 32.876.

17. See Li He's "Songs of the Bronze Immortal Bidding Farewell to Han" 金銅仙人辭漢歌: "The oxherd in the Wei palace points one thousand leagues off, / An acid gale from the Eastern Pass strikes the pupils of the eye." Cf. Frodsham, *Goddesses, Ghosts, and Demons*, 54.

18. These two lines are perhaps inspired by the ending of Li He's "Lady Li": "From out of the Jade Toad [a kind of clepsydra] water drips, / The Cock-herald chants. / Dewy flowers and orchid leaves / In dazzling disarray." Most of the poem is a mournful elegy for a palace lady, but these lines seem to take a more optimistic turn. See Frodsham, *Goddesses, Ghosts, and Demons*, 47.

19. These two lines seem to be inspired by Li He's "Someone I Love": "The qin's heart and the concubine's entrails / Both are severed this night, and both shall mend." Cf. Frodsham, *Goddesses, Ghosts, and Demons*, 215.

喝月曾驚群綠走	Calling on the moon, I'm startled to see the greens depart,[20]
飛香羞入叢紅宿	the wafting fragrance ashamed to join red petals.
少待有	Wait a little longer till
紫帳熱春雲	the purple canopy heats the spring clouds
楊花撲	and willow catkins brush past.[21]

---

    20. See Li He's "The King of Qin Drinks Wine" 秦王飲酒: "Intoxicated with wine, he calls on the moon till it walks backwards; / Silver clouds in serried ranks, the carnelian palace shines." Cf. Frodsham, *Goddesses, Ghosts, and Demons*, 44.

    21. See Li He's "Butterflies in Flight" 蝴蝶飛: "Willow catkins beat at the curtains under sweltering spring clouds" (Frodsham, *Goddesses, Ghosts, and Demons*, 124).

The Poetic Mind[22]

The poetic mind, in Jao's conception of it, is vast enough to encompass most of history yet always attentive to the slightest detail.

#1

詩心入冬眠	The mind of poetry sleeps at the coming of winter,
蜷臥遂三載	Its hibernation lasting three years.
言泉忽解泮	A torrent of words suddenly disperses,
一瀉到無外	Pouring out toward that beyond which is nothing.
好風枕上來	A fine breeze blows over my pillow,
咳唾拋亦快	Salivating phrases dispatched with relish.[23]
謝彼襤襪子	Tell all those shallow and slovenly souls:
名山今何在	Where today are the great mountains of the past?[24]

#2

有生無根蒂	We who were born yet lack roots or stems,[25]
有淚可朝宗	Having tears, let them converge to the source.[26]
處處皆牛山	Every place you go is always still Ox Mountain,[27]
那不傷道窮	So you cannot help but grieve that the Way is finished.
悠悠三千年	Across these three thousand years of the past,
孤憤一例同	The case of solitary indignation is the same throughout.
何如玉溪生	How much like what the Master of Jade Creek taught—[28]
且聽一樓鐘	Just keep listening for a bell from the tower.[29]

---

22. 詩心四首. *Wenji* 416.
23. Zhuangzi uses the figure of saliva as a complimentary term for speech or words. See *Zhuangzi* 31.1026 (cf. discussion of "Three Residues" in preface).
24. Historian Sima Qian said that one should hide books at famous mountains so that they would be preserved for posterity. See *Shi ji* 130.3320.
25. This line is based on one in a "Miscellaneous Poem" 雜詩 by Tao Qian. Cf. Hightower, *The Poetry of T'ao Ch'ien*, 185.
26. "Converge to the source" comes from the *Book of Documents*: "The Yangtze and the Han converge in the sea" 江漢朝宗於海. See *Shangshu zhengyi* 6.14a.
27. Lord Jing was visiting Ox Mountain, when he looked down over his capital and cried, lamenting that abrupt passage of human life. See *Liezi jishi* 6.213.
28. "Master of Jade Creek" was the sobriquet of Li Shangyin.
29. From a poem "Written on a Monk's Wall" 題僧壁 by Li Shangyin: "If one believes the words written on palm leaves [sutras] are true, / In all three lives you hear only the bell from the tower." See *Quan Tang shi* 539.6145–6146.

#3

愁陣奇兵出	Melancholy platoons and strange formations rise:[30]
其勢不可當	Their strength cannot be opposed.
以詩載之歸	I'll bring this home by means of a poem,
擲地聲鏗鏘	Thrown on the ground it makes a booming sound.[31]
吟賦非庾郎	Intoning rhapsodies I am no Gentleman Yu,[32]
避之身焉藏	Though I try to escape how can I conceal myself?
徒懷契闊心	In vain I bear this heart of long separation,
欲以問蒼蒼	Longing to inquire of the azure heavens.

#4

長夜悄然逝	The long night furtively departs,
林表麗朝暾	The woods' face is beautified by morning sun.
如彼溘死人	Like someone whose fate is sealed suddenly by death,
忽得見陽春	I see before me all at once the warmth of spring.
豹變此其時	This is the right time for the leopard to change its spots,[33]
游魂抑歸魂	Whether your soul is wandering away or returning.
寥寥天壤間	Of all the vastness between sky and earth,
待與智者論	I'd like to discuss this with someone wise.[34]

---

30. Han Wo 韓偓 (844–923) wrote: "Meditation subdues the devil of poetry, returning to the tranquil realm. / Wine assaults the formations of sadness, sending forth marvelous soldiers." See *Quan Tang shi* 681.7808.

31. This was said of a poem by Sun Chuo 孫綽 (314–371). See *Shishuo xinyu* 4/86.

32. Yu Xin 庾信 (513–581), who wrote the famous "Lament for the South," a long rhapsody lamenting the fall of the Liang dynasty.

33. In other words, the right time for a gentleman to write poetry. See *Changes*, hexagram #49, Ge 革: "The gentleman changes like a tiger. ... When the gentleman changes like a leopard, the patterns are resplendent" (*Zhou yi zhengyi* 5.20a).

34. The concluding line here recalls the conclusion of a poem by Xie Lingyun: "On All Four Sides of My New Dwelling at Stone Gate Are High Mountains, Winding Streams, Stony Cataracts, Lithe Bamboo, and Deep Forests." See Frodsham, *The Murmuring Stream*, 1: 136.

To the Tune of "Regret in the Damask Court"[35]

Yang Yucheng wrote me a letter saying, "Each time I read your *ci* poems, I am moved by their expression of pure literature." I replied with this poem.

玉笛猶纏窮思	Jade flutes still enfold dejected thoughts;
壓愁釅未醒	drinking to stop my sadness, I've not yet sobered up:
看過眼	I see pass before my eyes
士馬衣冠	gentlemen riders in robe and cap,
憑誰主	but who will serve as host,
畫壁旗亭	to inscribe the walls at Qi pavilion?[36]
十年題襟異國	For ten years writing of my inner feelings in an foreign country,
菁莪地	where "luxuriant grows the flixweed,"[37]
帶草仍量青	and bookstrap reeds are still faintly green;[38]
只去來	The seasons have come and gone
歲序侵尋	succeeding one another in order,
飄零客	while the traveler adrift
鬢變悲易盈	finds himself white-haired and prone to sorrow.

                 *   *   *

此去驛煙幾程	How many mists must you pass through to reach that post?
驚塵滿目	Dust abruptly fills my gaze,
況當萬里飛瓊	nephrite flurries over ten thousand miles:
寶瑟宵清	but my jeweled qin remains pristine through the night.
掩叢卷	Closing my accumulated scrolls,
忍重聽	how can I bear to listen again?

---

35. 綺寮怨. *Wenji* 609.
36. Referring to a story in which three High Tang poets, Wang Changling, Gao Shi 高適 (706–765), and Wang Zhihuan 王之渙 (688–742), listened to a performance of singing girls, making a mark on the wall each time their own poems were sung. See *Ji yi ji,* 12b–14a.
37. The title of *Odes* 176. According to the Mao preface, the poem describes a state whose sovereign fosters talent.
38. The classical scholar Zheng Xuan 鄭玄 (127–200, style name Kangcheng 康成) used a certain plant with broad leaves to make a strap for his books, and the local people called it the "Kangcheng bookstrap." See *San Qi ji* 三齊記, quoted in *Hou Han shu* 112/22.3475n6.

堪嘆惜陰人去	Lament the precious hours and men who have departed:
珍重閣	it is that scholar of Cherished Greatness[39]
最傷情	I grieve for most today.
歌翻渭城	I play the "Weicheng" tune,[40]
相從恨歲晚	Together we regret the season is late,
空涕零	shedding empty tears.

---

39. Zhenzhongge 珍重閣, roughly translated as "Scholar of Cherished Greatness," was a sobriquet of Zhao Zunyue 趙尊嶽 (1898–1965), *ci* poet and teacher, who collaborated with Jao.

40. "Weicheng" is an alternate title for the song "Yangguan" 陽關. Jao's note: I used to study *ci* and music with Shuyong (Zhao Zunyue), and we would discuss the Ming-dynasty tune "Yangguan."

To the Tune of "Passing the Towers of Qin"[41]

Poetry is a potent form of consolation for what has been lost.

夢切江雲	I dreamt I cut a cloud from the river to keep
恨抽芳草	and coveted the fragrant grasses,
霧澀剪秋難斷	but the fog was too bland to cut, the autumn hard to sever.
斜陽屋底	Sunlight slanting on the roof,
猶挾餘寒	I am still struck by the lingering cold.
世上久拋紈扇	I long ago lost a gauze fan out there.
惆悵老去填詞	Sad to have grown old I still compose lyrics,
偏愛良宵	loving above all the midnight,
怕催銀箭	afraid to hurry time's silver arrows.[42]
看屏山曲曲	Looking over each crook and nook of the mountain screen,
孤燈無語	these solitary lamps cannot speak
水涯人遠	to you there beyond the seas.

* * *

誰問訊	Should someone ask
酒面紅生	why my face is flushed with wine,
酬春無力	I lack the power to requite the spring,
暖入碧波濃染	whose warmth enters infusing emerald waves.
冰澌老巷	Ice thawing in familiar alleys,
風掩重門	wind slams the double gates,
一夜鬢霜先變	in one night my temples are transformed by frost.
冷句飛香	Chilled phrases and fleeting fragrance:[43]
重怪他	I always blame them,
清露時搓	while brushed occasionally by pure dew,
浮萍難倩	unable to rely on the floating duckweed.
想天孫此際無睡	I think of the Weaving Girl sleepless in Heaven[44]
星如淚點	where the stars look like teardrops.

---

41. 過秦樓. *Wenji* 622.
42. The silver arrows pointing to the time in a clepsydra.
43. Adapted from Jiang Kui's *ci* to the tune of "Charms of Niannu" on enjoying lotus blossoms: "Shaken and tossed alluringly, / Cold fragrance flies on my verses." Cf. Lin, *The Transformation of the Chinese Lyrical Tradition*, 130.
44. The star Vega, said to be separated from the Cowherd star Altair except for at the Qixi 七夕 festival (Japanese Tanabata) when the two are reunited.

X
On Scholarship

Jao is a Renaissance man, excelling in various fields of endeavor that are normally treated as separate compartments without any overlap. Probably the most striking feature of his polymathy, though, is the way that Jao combines creative and critical work. As Jao reflects in one essay: "This seems to be an age when scholarship and art are entirely separated. Since specialized scholarship began, it has been held distinct from artistic expression."[1] But this broader trend toward specialization has not confined Jao's own creativity, as he integrates scholarship and poetic expression.

---

1. *Rao Zongyi ershi shiji xueshu wenji* 18:362.

To the Tune of "Lips Dotted with Rouge": For My Chuci Bibliography[2]

One of Jao's many fields of scholarship was on the classic anthology Chuci, *allusions to which are also integrated into his whole poetic oeuvre. This poem focuses on the mournful quality of the anthology, alluding also the many fragrant plants that appear there as symbols of the poet's virtue.*

一片騷心	Chu elegies in my heart,
雨昏閶闔天長閉	on a rainy night the Gate of Heaven stays shut.
故鄉臨眺	When I gaze back at my old home now,
城郭非耶是	Even the walls are no longer the same.[3]

* * *

鵜鳩聲聲	With every cry of the cuckoo,[4]
目極心千里	my heart's vision extends one thousand leagues away.[5]
南枝倚	Perching on southern branches,
滿江蘭芷	The river is blooming with orchids and angelica:
待得春風起	I wait for the spring wind to come.

---

2. 點絳唇・自題楚辭書錄. *Wenji* 573. Composed for Jao's own bibliography of scholarship on the classic anthology of poems, *Chuci*.

3. Ding Lingwei is said to have transformed into an immortal crane, and sang a song lamenting that although the walls of his hometown were the same, the people of his day were all gone. See *Yiwen leiju* 78.1331.

4. In the "Li sao" the cry of the cuckoo is associated with the coming of autumn and the withering of plants. See *Chuci buzhu* 1.39.

5. This line paraphrases the famous concluding lines of "Summons to the Soul." See *Chuci buzhu* 9.215.

To the Tune of "Butterflies in Love with Flowers": For My Painting on the Translation of *Dream of a Red Chamber* by David Hawkes[6]

David Hawkes' translation of the classic novel under the title Story of a Stone *was one of the great Sinological achievements of the twentieth century, as Jao recognized.*

身世落花春苦護	Spring fiercely guards the fallen blossoms of our lives:
雨點風痕	Raindrops and traces of wind,
紙墨斑斕處	dots of ink scattered on paper.
夢裏杜鵑君解語	Only you can understand the message of the cuckoo in the dream,
不辭百計留春住	Not sparing a hundred schemes to make the springtime stay.

* * *

異代知音宜細訴	You should carefully instruct an understanding friend from another age:
樓外飛花	The blossoms swirling outside the mansion
鎮是春歸路	are ever the path by which spring departs.
筆縱生花誰惜取	Should this brush create flowers, who would begrudge that you take them?
隨他夢逐天涯去	I'd follow his dream up to the edge of Heaven.

---

6. 蝶戀花・題紅樓譯書圖為霍客思作. *Wenji* 656.

Essay on Crabs[7]

Through its use of carefully selected allusions, this light poem in the fu *genre makes of the humble crab a symbolic vessel for the aspirations of Chinese civilization. The poem is such a feast of erudition that it seems fitting to place it together with Jao's other literary celebrations of scholarship. It must have been composed before 1963, since it was written for Pu Xinshe 溥心畬 (1896–1963), a member of the imperial family of the Qing dynasty and a prominent painter. He had fled to Taiwan in 1949, but when visiting Hong Kong he said that he had come specifically to try the crabs. The majority of allusions in the poem refer to amusing anecdotes from the Han or Jin dynasties, but the poem also mentions the historical use of crabs in lacquer production and concludes with a celebration of Song-dynasty painting. Thus the poem as a whole modulates between different fields of human experience: history, literature, and art, not to mention the world of the crabs themselves.*

渺江南之煙水	Far away the misty waters of Jiangnan
分翠色於菰蒲	Have halcyon hues distinct from the water bamboo and cattails.
違春荷與夏槿	Unlike the spring lotus and the summer hibiscus,
及秋杪而冬初	Their prime is autumn's end and winter's beginning.
5 看荻花之爭白	Look at the reeds and blossoms vying for whiteness,
紛蜋螘以競趨	A crowd of female crabs striving to advance.[8]
殘沙斷岸	Lingering on the sands, dividing the banks,
短日平蕪	They pass brief days on the overgrown plain.
沉清光於沼沚	Sinking pure light in the swamps and pools,
10 狎蒹葭之尺鳧	They play amid the reeds with the footlong ducks.
含黃可繪	Those "bearers of yellow roe" can paint,
無腹而驅	The "stomachless" crabs chase one another.
何曾化漆	Why were they once made into lacquer,[9]
但取胼膚	Using only their tough shells?
15 半炊則沒林於水	Half-cooked, they are like a forest submerged in water,
一舉或十里專車	Lifted out they would fill a car ten miles long.
索轉帶於張揖	Search for the female crabs with Zhang Yi,[10]
閱貢物於周書	Peruse the tribute goods in the *Documents of Zhou*.

---

7. 蟹賦. *Wenji* 277; *Gu'an wenlu* 8.

8. *Gu'an wenlu* has 䂿 for 蜋. *Lang yi* 蜋螘 is a term for female crabs (see *Guang ya shuzheng* 10B.28a).

9. Crabs were used in lacquer production, though there were different theories about which part of the crab's body made the key contribution. See "Stabilized Lacquer Latex and Perpetual Youth," in Needham, *Science and Civilisation in China*, vol. 5, part 4, pp. 207–210.

10. This term for female crabs also derives from the *Guang ya* (see note to line 6 above). This was the encyclopedia compiled by Zhang Yi in the third century.

	覺萬螯之生涼	Noticing their myriad pincers feel a chill,
20	感歲時之云徂	They sense the seasons of the year are passing.
	甘拍浮於酒池	I would rather paddle in a pool of wine[11]
	了一世之賢愚	Than live out this age of wise men and fools.
	慚爾雅之不熟	I regret not being more familiar with the *Erya*,[12]
	信王據之足誅	Trust that Wang Shu deserved execution.[13]
25	持盃壯畢氏之豪	Raising a cup, I praise the boldness of Master Bi,
	獨烹哂張敞之迂	Cooking alone, I laugh at Zhang Chang's pedantry.[14]
	甕供吏部之醉	Vats provide for the intoxication of the Minister of Personnel;[15]
	糟有靈均之餔	The dregs are all that is left for Lingjun to sup on.[16]
	假丹青於惠崇	Borrow the crimson and green from Hui Chong,[17]
30	極神麗於伯駒	Achieve the divine loveliness of a Boju.[18]
	比蓴羹乎千里	When you compare the mallow soup one thousand leagues away,[19]
	永相忘於江湖	You can at last forget yourself in the lakes and rivers.[20]

---

11. Bi Zhuo 畢卓 drank himself into a stupor amid his neighbor's wine vats and was mistaken for a thief. He once said: "If I could obtain a boat full of several hundreds of *hu* of wine, and the finest delicacies of the four seasons on both sides, then with a goblet of wine in my right hand, and a crab claw in my left, I would paddle and float along in my ship of wine, and so live out my life." See *Jin shu* 49.1381. Bi Zhuo is referred to again below in lines 25–28.

12. Cai Mo 蔡謨 (281–356) mistook the fiddler crab (family *Ocypodidae*) for the edible kind, based on his recollection of the *Quan xue* 勸學 by his own ancestor Cai Yong 蔡邕 ("the crab has eight legs, plus two pincers"). The earlier dictionary *Erya* 爾雅 had distinguished the poisonous fiddler crab (*peng qi* 蜂蜞) from the edible version. Xie Shang told Cai, "Because you did not read *Erya* thoroughly, you were nearly killed by *Quan xue*." See *Jin shu* 77.2041.

13. Wang Shu was executed for not providing fish and crabs. See *Jin shu* 102.2661.

14. Zhang Chang (?–51 BCE) was a Western Han official. In a letter to Zhu Deng 朱登, he thanks him for his gift of crab paste, and says that he enjoyed it with three friends, since Qu Boyu 蘧伯玉 had done the same with a gift from Confucius. See Yan Kejun, "Quan Han wen" 全漢文, in *Quan shanggu Sandai Qin Han Sanguo Liuchao wen*, 30.6a/b.

15. The Minister of Personnel is Bi Zhuo from line 21.

16. Lingjun refers to Qu Yuan. In the "Fisherman" chapter of the *Chuci*, a fisherman counsels Qu Yuan to compromise with his rivals at court, "supping on the dregs" alongside them.

17. Hui Chong 惠崇 (967–1017) was a Northern Song monk-painter.

18. Zhao Boju 趙伯駒 was a Southern Song painter.

19. Zhang Han 張翰 (fl. 301–312) was serving the court in Luoyang when one day the autumn breeze made him think of the "water bamboo, mallow soup, and diced perch" in his native place of Wu (modern Suzhou). He left immediately and returned home. See *Jin shu* 92.2384.

20. "When the spring is dried up, the fish may try to survive on land, breathing on each other to keep wet, soaking each other with bubbles, but it really would be better to forget themselves in the rivers and lakes." See *Zhuangzi* 6.242.

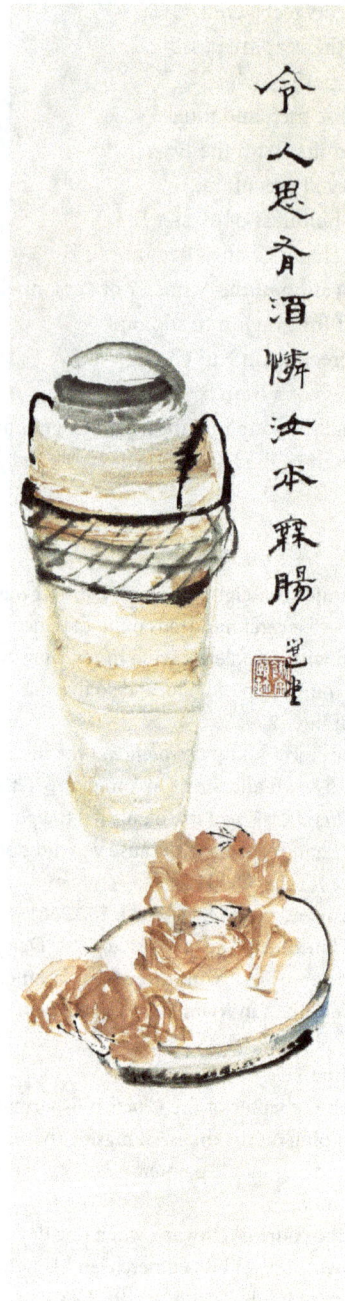

Illustration 10. *Crab and Wine* (1991).

Encomium for the Mawangdui Silk Manuscript of the *Book of Changes*[21]

Throughout his career one of Jao's main preoccupations has been the study of excavated texts and other rare manuscripts. He has particularly emphasized the role that these texts, which provided a rare unmediated glimpse into the culture of ancient China, should play in contemporary understanding of ancient Chinese civilization and thought. Some of the most remarkable discoveries have come from the Mawangdui site in Changsha, excavated in the early 1970s. With this poem composed in the tetrasyllabic form of the ancient *Book of Odes* (employing only a single rhyme throughout), Jao celebrates the manuscript of the *Book of Changes* found at this site.

	易本卜筮	The *Changes* were originally used for divination,
	未遭秦殃	And so avoided the cataclysm of Qin;[22]
	楚始子弓	In Chu it was Zigong first
	傳自魯商	Who had learned it from Lu Shang.[23]
5	王臣蹇蹇	"The King's officers are loyal and honest,"[24]
	正則佩纕	Zhengze adorned himself with pendants.[25]
	蘭陵非相	Lanling wrote "Repudiating Physiognomy,"[26]
	語述括囊	Enclosing all the statements and commentary.

---

21. 馬王堆帛書易經贊. *Wenji* 296. Jao's preface: A silk manuscript of the *Book of Changes* (*Yijing*) was excavated from tomb #3 at Mawangdui in Changsha. It includes all the sixty-four hexagrams from first to last, it is not divided into halves, lacks the *tuan* [Decision] and *xiang* [Image] sections, and has numerous textual variants relative to the received text. Even the names of the Hexagrams are different, for instance, Qian is Jian, Lü as Li, etc.; I cannot list all the discrepancies here. Also, the "Commentary to the Appended Statements" is basically the same as that of the received text, though it lacks several paragraphs on "Da yan," including the first three paragraphs of "Explicating the Hexagrams." There are also 2,100 characters not seen in the extant *Changes*. One section is called "Zhao li," another "1,638." Du Yu's postface to the *Collected Commentaries to the Zuo Tradition* says: "The text from the Ji tumulus has an additional 'Explication of Yin and Yang,' but lacks the 'Decisions,' 'Image Statements,' 'Words of the Text,' and 'Appended statements.'" This seems very close to the case here. I had the opportunity to examine a reproduction of the entire manuscript at the Hunan Provincial Museum. I look forward to its official publication and for now just give a general description to record my good fortune at seeing it, along with the following encomium.

22. The burning of Confucian texts by the First Emperor of Qin.

23. Lu Shangqu 魯商瞿 (in the Chinese text his name is abbreviated to two characters to fit the meter) is said to have received *Yijing* learning from Confucius. See *Shi ji* 121.3127.

24. This line is a quotation from the text of hexagram #39, Jian 蹇 (*Zhou yi zhengyi* 4.22b).

25. Zhengze is one of Qu Yuan's sobriquets, given in the "Li sao," *Chuci buzhu* 1.1.

26. Xunzi 荀子 was magistrate of Lanling in Chu.

	陸賈思務	Lu Jia wrote "Thinking of Diligence,"[27]
10	豐蔀是詳	Knew in detail of the "curtain of such fullness."[28]
	淮南九師	There were nine masters in Huainan,
	說也久亡	But their explications have long been lost.
	繄此帛書	Oh, this writing upon silk!
	鬆匰內藏	It was preserved inside a lacquer box,
15	界以朱絲	Tied with vermilion silk,
	篆籀成行	Its lines composed of seal script old and new.[29]
	漢志所載	As recorded in the *Han Annals*,
	易繇陰陽	The *Changes* originate in the principles of Yin and Yang.[30]
	汲冢古文	In the Old Text manuscripts from Ji tumulus,
20	彖象則喪	The "Decisions" and "Image Statements" were lost.
	與此差同	The differences and similarities with this text
	可以頡頏	Can be compared and evaluated.
	復有昭力	Then there is the "Power to Illuminate,"[31]
	研討未遑	Which has not yet been investigated and understood.
25	繫辭不分	The "Appended Statements" are not placed separately,
	挩其篇章	And some of those passages have been lost.
	說卦後得	"Explicating the Hexagrams" was obtained later,
	厥說可商	And its interpretations may be challenged.
	借鍵為健	It uses a loangraph for "Jian,"
30	未知孰長	But who knows which version is superior?
	以柫為否	It uses the character *fou* instead of "not,"
	義待衡量	Whose meaning still deserves to be considered.
	似中古文	Though similar to ancient writing,
	其肻非常	The character *hui* is out of the ordinary.
35	無咎未脫	"Without blame" has not been omitted,[32]
	費氏所言	Though Master Fei was ignorant of this.[33]
	太卜三易	The Grand Diviner had three *Changes*,
	筮亦多方	The ways of prognostication were many.

---

27. Lu Jia (240–170 BCE) was a scholar and political thinker from Chu.
28. "Curtain of such fullness," referring to an eclipse, may be found in the text of hexagram #55, Feng 豐. See Wilhelm-Baynes 214; *Zhou yi zhengyi* 6.2b.
29. *Zhuan* 篆 is seal script, and *zhou* 籀 refers to the older form of seal script associated with Confucius, also known as "major seal script" 大篆.
30. This alludes to Han minister Bing Ji's 丙吉 remarks, quoted in *Han shu* 74.3139.
31. "Power to illuminate" is a section without parallel in the received texts.
32. "Without blame" is often used in the line statements of the *Changes*.
33. Fei Zhi 費直 was a Western Han scholar of the *Changes*.

	睹斯瓌奇	Perceiving this marvelous treasure,[34]
40	挹古芬芳	We partake of an ancient fragrance.
	比物取象	Comparing the objects to select the image,
	昭冥愈狂	What once was dark is illuminated ever faster.
	本隱之顯	The text originally obscure has been revealed,
	潛德復光	Its concealed virtue shining forth once more.
45	三絕韋編	Thrice snapped the leather binding of the bamboo strips,[35]
	義須發皇	That their meaning could be elucidated further.
	敢告來賢	What can we tell the scholars of the future,
	誦之勿忘	But to recite it over again, and never to forget?[36]

---

34. Here 賭 is emended from 睹.

35. The binding snapped while Confucius was diligently perusing his copy of the *Changes*. See *Han shu* 88.3589.

36. A similar phrase is used in Zheng Xuan's commentary to *Odes* 269. See *Mao shi zhengyi* 19A.19a.

XI

Dreams

Dreams and their symbolism are central to Jao's aesthetic thought. He likes to quote Jung: "A great work of art is like a dream; for all its apparent obviousness it does not explain itself and is never equivocal." In the preface to Jao's collection of lyrics Gu'an ci, *Jao discusses his theory of* ci, *which applies well to his poetry and aesthetics in general, and explains the importance of dreams to all his creative writings:*[1]

Ci are different from *shi* poems. Because they are intricately twisted, they can communicate what is obscure; because they are lofty and bold, they can penetrate what is distant. The heart has a longing for the realm of the obscure: the mind of the *ci* ferments there, and when the emotion can no longer be borne, it creates an impulse distinct as the point of a blade. Zhou Bangyan said: "From many worries, only the feeling of a single instant remains. As the worries grow deeper each day, the feeling stays. When they are released for a moment, that is the right occasion." Whether the finest lines are achieved must depend upon the author's talent and experience, but there is no way to control all that. When I was young I was fond of writing lyrics, but since I went into flight in the southwest, far removed from everything, though I did not lose my inspiration and passion, I did cease writing for a while. Since coming to Hong Kong nearly twenty years ago, I have occasionally returned to lyrics. At dawn or at dusk, facing the cycle of creation and destruction, through the inspiration of painting and the mind of meditation, I have written of a single moment's feeling. The rivers and mountains where I lived, and the storms and tempests I experienced, have increased my sense of sorrow. Trimming and editing these poems I have compiled them into one scroll. I hope this is not a pointless task, so long as I have expressed something of the passions of my life.

---

1. *Wenji* 568.

Lyrics should aim for the transparent and empty,[2] the sense beyond the surface of words. I cherish the new but speak of the remote to comfort my migrant soul. I clutch to a candle as the spring deepens, as if to warm again a dream of the past.

---

2. See Zhang Yan's 張炎 (1248–1320) theory of the *ci*: "The *ci* must be transparent and empty, not substantive and solid: if it is transparent and empty, then it can be classical and elegant, powerful and daring; but if it is too substantive and solid, then it will become clotted and harsh, obscuring the flavor" (*Ci yuan* B.6a).

To the Tune of "Fragrant Grass Waves": Recording a Dream[3]

Jao's dream poems depict a feeling so ineffable it could hardly exist outside of verse.

甚一霎	In this instant
便再覓華胥	I see again that dreamland of Huaxu,[4]
更紫帡千種愁心	Under the purple canopy is my heart of one thousand sorrows,
欲付行雨	I'd like to entrust it to the driving rain.
休道吟愫苦	Don't say that singing of my bitter suffering
同蛩吟低訴	Is just like the crickets' low stridulation.
海氣近	Approaching mirages
換盡朝昏	I'll exchange the daylight hours
暮靄來去	to pass my time in twilight haze.

               *   *   *

空覷	I watch absent-mindedly
燕梁藻井	The swallow roofbeams in the caisson ceiling:
縱返銜泥難覓路	even if they went to bear mud for their nests they could not find the way.
問可有	I ask could there be
驚烏屋角	a startled crow on the rafters
窺人舊庭戶	observing the old house there,
翠裙百幅	One hundred lengths of halcyon skirts,
浣不盡涉江情緒	the feeling of Qu Yuan "crossing the river" that cannot be purged.[5]
怕瘦柳	I tremble for the lithe willows
月出參差又舞	that move once more in motley dance to the moonlight.

---

   3. 芳草波・紀夢. *Wenji* 634.
   4. "Huaxu" is the utopian world described in *Liezi jishi* 2.41.
   5. "Crossing the River" is one of the "Nine Pieces" in the *Chuci* which describe Qu Yuan's exile.

To the Tune of "Washing Creek Sands"[6]

Fresh willows shooting forth their buds, as they reflect the sunlight, take on a golden color. Alongside the road these look exquisitely lovely.

感激東風逐積寒	Grateful for the East Wind that dispatches long-borne chills,
暫攜午夢去長安	I'll carry a noontime dream with me from Chang'an.
冶條嬌小露初乾	The twining branches are tender and lithe under dewdrops barely dry.

* * *

雪減一分晴更好	When the snow begins to melt the clear scene is all the finer.
鴉藏千縷地常寬	Crows hide in the thousand wisps of willow, the earth extends without limit.
赤欄橋畔繫征鞍	On the red railing by the bridge, I fix my saddle for a new journey.

---

6. 浣溪沙. *Wenji* 627.

To the Tune of "Bitter Longing"[7]

Composed in his head during a long car trip, after the model of a classic Qing dynasty poem, Jao spells out a new variation on the venerable theme "Où sont les neiges d'antan?" The sites mentioned belong to the heartland of ancient Chinese culture in the Yellow River basin, located in modern Henan province.

古往今來征戰路	From the past up to the present moment this has been a road of conquest:
更千里	Another one thousand miles of
桑榆樹	mulberry and elm trees.
算眼底	In the vista before me
雄關紛可數	the mighty passes are too many to be counted.
虎牢也	Tiger pen, ah![8]
知何處	where is it now?
轘轅也	Huanyuan, ah![9]
知何處	where is it now?

* * *

長河渺渺公無渡	The yellow river extends to the horizon; you should not cross it!
休更作	Don't write any more
溫韋語	those verses of Wen and Wei.[10]
指宋苑	Behold those estates of Song:
梁園誰信據	who now occupies those Liang gardens?[11]
秋水也	The floods of autumn, ah!
隨雲去	are gone with the clouds;
秋雁也	The geese of autumn, ah!
隨人去	are gone with those men.

---

7. 酷相思. *Wenji* 759. Jao's preface: Li Zhi 李贄 (1686–1762), "the man who mourned the Way," once copied out a lyric by Chen Weisong 陳維崧 (1625–1682). Riding a car on the way to Xingyang 滎陽 (in Henan province), I recited it to myself silently, and playfully composed these verses matching the rhymes.

8. A frontier strongpoint to the west of Xingyang county.

9. A mountain pass southeast of Yanshi 偃師 county, Henan.

10. Lyrics by Wen Tingyun 溫庭筠 (812–870) and Wei Zhuang 韋莊 (10th c.).

11. The gardens of Liang (the ancient state located in the area of modern Henan) were famous because Liu Wu 劉武 (184–144 BCE), Prince of Liang during the Han dynasty, built a magnificent garden there for his court.

To the Tune of "Jade Mansion Spring"[12]

When Jao closes his eyes a vision of "the whole sky" appears.

浮生未合江南住	In this floating life I have never been able to live in the Southland;
桃梗任飄留夢處	Like those peach figurines ever adrift, abiding only in the place of dreams.[13]
回頭十載霎時情	Looking back through these ten years, just an instant of feeling,
合眼一天芳草路	I close my eyes and the whole sky becomes a flower-strewn path.

* * *

煙檻撼雪飛無數	The mist-drawn lattice is shaken by snow in random flurries.
簾葦漾風搖翠暮	Bamboo and reeds are borne up in the wind, which stirs the turquoise dusk.
有愁此際轉無愁	Just as I begin to feel melancholy it turns into not having melancholy;[14]
獨臥珠幢聽墜絮	Sleeping alone under a pearl canopy I hear the willow floss in its flight.

---

12. 玉樓春. *Wenji* 629.

13. In the Warring States era, when Meng Changjun 孟嘗君 was going to visit the state of Qin, Su Dai 蘇代 persuaded him not to go by telling him an allegory about people made of clay and people made of wood: the former are buried by a flood but can return to the earth, while the latter are swept away in the current. See *Zhanguo ce jianzheng* 10.588–589.

14. As in Li Shangyin's "Northern Qi Dynasty Song: Melody without Melancholy, But Melancholy Still" 無愁果有愁曲北齊歌 (*Quan Tang shi* 540.6204).

Playful Rhymes on Traveling to the Moon[15]

This poem exhibits the more playful side of Jao's writing, as he imagines being on the moon with a number of classic mythological figures.

#1

靜海翻雲黑似烏	The Sea of Tranquility turns over clouds black as crows.
再來初地已模糊	Returning to their primal ground they are already indistinct.[16]
廣寒宮裏銀河路	Inside the Palace of Boundless Chill, on the road to the Silver River;[17]
飛雪揚塵始戒途	Only when snow falls on the dusty seas do we begin the journey.[18]

#2

吳質肯將桂樹拋	Is Wu Zhi willing to depart the cassia tree?[19]
蟾蜍散盡恐難遭	The toads have all dispersed and may not be met again.
人間鑿險俄天上	Mankind courts danger there in the precipitous heavens;[20]
此去雲霄幾羽毛	Up there in the cloud-laced ether, how many birds survive?[21]

---

15. 登月戲詠. *Wenji* 527.
16. The "primal ground" is the first of the ten stages of a Bodhisattva's path to enlightenment.
17. The Palace of Boundless Chill was located on the moon, according to Daoist cosmology.
18. Jao depicts the moon as the home of the immortals, who live so much longer than mortal beings that "the seas begin to raise up dust." See *Taiping guangji* 60.370.
19. The moon god Wu Gong 吳剛, as in Li He's poem "Prelude: Li Ping at the Vertical Harp" 李憑箜篌引: "Wu Zhi, still awake, leans on a cassia tree, / As dew drops fly aslant, drenching the hare with cold." See Frodsham, *Goddesses, Ghosts, and Demons*, 3.
20. "Courts danger" is literally "chiseling into danger," as in Yuan Mei's 袁枚 (1716–1797) phrase "chiseling into danger and hoisting the mysterious" 鑿險縋幽.
21. Literally "how many feathers," as in Du Fu's "Singing of My Cares at an Ancient Ruin" 詠懷古跡: "In the cloud-laced ether of ten thousand ages a single feather." See *Du shi xiangzhu* 17.1506.

Dreaming of Return[22]

A regulated octet from Jao's collection "Ice and Charcoal."

頻年惟夢以為歸	Through these many years it is only in dream that I return,
夢繞故山日幾圍	Dreams circle those hills of my old home many times a day.
鵲噪妻孥驚我在	Magpies chittering, my wife and babe are startled to find me there,[23]
鴻飛城郭覺今非	For wild geese soaring past the city walls everything is different now.[24]
天留世棄同無妄	Heaven has preserved me and the world abandoned me equally without reason;
海立山頹豈式微	The oceans stay, the mountains crumble, but how can I return?[25]
賸有茫茫游子意	All that's left is this one wanderer cast adrift
八千里外念庭闈	Eight thousand miles away, thinking of my parents' courtyard.

---

22. 夢歸. *Wenji* 544.

23. Cf. Du Fu's poem "Qiang Village" 羌村, #1: "My wife and children find it strange that I survive, / Startled in place they wipe away their tears." See *Du shi xiangzhu* 5.391.

24. Ding Lingwei 丁令威 is said to have transformed into an immortal crane, and sang a song lamenting that although the walls of his hometown were the same, the people of his day were all gone. See *Yiwen leiju* 78.1331.

25. See *Odes* 36: "Decline, decline, / Why not return?"

To the Tune of "The Beauty Yu": On Not Seeing the Moon at Mid-Autumn 1955[26]

The following ci *poem describes an unusual situation: the moon is concealed by clouds on the very night of the Mid-Autumn festival, when one is supposed to look up at the full moon and think of one's friends or family in faraway places all enjoying it at the same time.*

年年呵凍荒池水	Year after year I blow upon the chilled inkpot to soften it,
滴滴成新淚	drop by drop forming new tears:
今宵忽見月華明	tonight all at once I saw the gleam of the full moon.
咫尺鄉關	Home seems only inches away
竟是百年程	though in fact one hundred years' journey.

*   *   *   **

叢篁山鬼休相怪	Mountain spirits in the bamboo thickets, don't blame me!
窈窕人安在	Where has that fair lady gone?
不知秋色在誰家	I wonder whose home enjoys an autumn scene tonight?
露腳斜飛	Dewdrops falling aslant
又被碧雲遮	are blocked in turn by the gemlike clouds.

---

26. 虞美人：乙未中秋不見月. *Wenji* 573.

Waking Up from Sleep[27]

Zhuangzi dreamed he was a butterfly, but then when he awoke was no longer sure if he was Zhuangzi who had dreamed he was a butterfly, or a butterfly dreaming it was Zhuangzi.

心花開到落梅前	My heart-flowers bloom just before the plum blossoms fall,[28]
清夢深藏五百年	A pure dream that contains five centuries within it.
蝴蝶何曾迷遠近	Was ever butterfly lost between the near and the far?
眼中歷歷是山川	Before my gaze those same mountains and rivers are clearly visible.

---

27. 睡起. *Wenji* 516.
28. For "heart-flowers" cf. "Cheung Chau Collection #18" in section IX above.

Dreaming of Heaven[29]

The title references a classic poem by Li He.

夜夢捫天萬疊青	In nighttime's dreams I touch the myriad folds of azure Heaven,
弛魂何遠叩冥冥	My soul reposing in remote inquires of the great void there.
千年走馬人間世	One thousand years pass like a stallion racing past this human realm,
但覺乾坤水上萍	And I feel Earth and Sky are merely duckweed skimming the water.

---

29. 夢天. *Wenji* 517.

Illustration 11. *Scenery of Southern China* (2004).

To the Tune of "Fragrance of Angelica and Orchid Prelude": On Shadow[30]

Nietzsche discussed how to evade the tumult of the world, and said that men who could do likewise are just like shadows. As the sun descends to the west the shadows grow ever larger. Only their humility is like the setting of the sun, which can keep to the darkness, fearing only the interference of the light.[31] This is similar to Zhuangzi's saying about concealing and thereby preserving one's own brilliance.[32] Here I develop this theme.

清吹峭煙	A clear breeze in the misty peaks
拂明鏡	brushes the limpid mirror:
恥隨雞鶩	I am ashamed to consort with mere chickens and ducks.
看夕照西斜	Looking at the sunset rays sinking in the west,
林隙照人更綠	the reflection through the forest gaps is greener still.
水平雁散	Over level waters the geese disperse,
又鎮日相隨金屋	and chase one another all day past golden mansions.
自憩陰別後	Since the parting I rest in the shade,
悄倚無言修竹	leaning mutely against the tall bamboo.

              *   *   *

火日相屯	As the fiery days accumulate
陰宵互代	dark nights follow in turn[33]
可異涼燠	opposing cold and warmth.
況露電飛花	Even with the dew, lightning, and scattered blossoms[34]
難寫暫乖欷曲	it is hard to describe the feeling of brief separation.
江山寥落	The rivers and mountains are utterly bare
白雲滿目	as white clouds fill my gaze:
但永秋遙夜	Only eternal autumn and everlasting night
伴余幽獨	accompany me in hidden solitude.

---

30. 蕙蘭芳引 影. *Wenji* 616; *Ershi shiji shi da jia ci xuan* 291–292.
31. *Genealogy of Morals*, 3rd Essay, Section VIII. Nietzsche is discussing the "philosopher" who shrinks away from "fame, princes, and women."
32. See *Zhuangzi* 2.83.
33. Cf. *Zhuangzi* 27.960.
34. These images for impermanence derive from the *Diamond Sutra, T* 235: 8.752b.

To the Tune of "Spring Resentment in the Boudoir"[35]

Among the Dunhuang airs, I most relish the *Yun yao ji* 雲謠集 (Cloud song collection). While I was in Paris I saw, on the reverse of a scroll of the ancient-text *Book of Documents*, two songs to the tune "Longing for a Man of Yue" and one "Spring Resentment in the Boudoir," the lyrics of which read:

好天良夜月	In fair weather and mild nights the moon
碧宵高挂	is suspended high in emerald skies.
羞對文鸞	Demure before the phoenix mirror,[36]
淚濕紅羅帕	her tears wetting the red gauze handkerchief.
時斂愁眉	Now knitting her sorrowful brows
恨君顛罔	she hates her lord for his betrayals;
夜夜歸來	night after night at his return
紅燭長流雲榭	red lamps gutter along in the cloudy pavilions.

* * *

夜久更深	As the night grows deeper
羅帳虛薰蘭麝	the space of gauze curtains is scented with orchid and musk.
頻頻出戶	Often she sets out through the door
迎取嘶嘶馬	to meet the neighing horse.
含笑闈	Holding in a laugh,
輕輕罵	with just a light rebuke,
把衣搏搶	She tugs at his clothes and drags him in.
叵奈金枝	How troublesome the waning candelabra;
扶入水晶簾下	she helps him in under the canopy of crystal.

The latter song had not been recorded elsewhere, so I showed it to Professor Demiéville, who was pleased enough to translate it into French. It reads like spring wind on a fragrant path or like a beautiful woman from Yue; the extract is beautiful as fine brocade, an equal to the pieces in *Among the Flowers* [the Five Dynasties *ci* collection]. I have written this short poem matching its rhymes, to celebrate this immortal composition.

---

35. 怨春閨. *Wenji* 586. There is a French translation of the first song by Demiéville in his collaborative publication with Jao on the Dunhuang songs. See *Airs de Touen-huang* 112.

36. The *luanjing* 鸞鏡 is an elegant term for a mirror. According to a story reported in the preface to a poem by Fan Tai 范泰 (355–), the King of Kashmir, concerned that his pet phoenix was lonely after it refused to sing for three years, set up a mirror to give it the illusion of company. Instead it cried out sadly and died. See *Taiping yulan* 916.2b.

江山經雨洗	The rivers and mountains are swept by rain,
疏桐蟾掛	the toad-moon suspended in sparse paulownia.
誰與蘭香	Who can share the orchid fragrance,
借取秋雲帕	borrow a handkerchief of autumn cloud?
垂蕊銀燈	Silver lamps dangling wax blossoms,
休驚夢短	don't be startled the dream is short
斜墜芳鈿	and the fragrant hairpin falls askew;
彈淚彩箋虛榭	brush your tears from the love note you received in the empty pavilion.

悄悄人歸	Silently he returns,
冉冉流蘇沉麝	slowly trailing tassels scented with musk.
千金片刻	This moment is worth one thousand pieces of gold,
換足五花馬	as much as a five-hued horse.[37]
含笑指	Smirking and pointing,
春禽罵	spring birds mock,
好風輕搚	A fine breeze lightly tugging his sleeve:
珍護紅心	Cherish that crimson heart,
步入碧桃花下	step in under the flowering peach blossoms.[38]

---

37. See Li Bai's "Bringing in the Wine": "Five-hued horse, thousand ingot purse" (*Li Taibai quanji* 3.180).

38. The *bitao* 碧桃 peach is frequently used as a symbol of a lover's bower.

To the Tune of "Flower-Strewn Path": On Red Tea[39]

Chinese red tea is normally called black tea in English, but this poem employs the color imagery according to the Chinese term.

星依北渚雲	Stars follow the clouds of the northern islet,
春在東闌雪	spring arrives in the snow of the eastern gate.
空園凋蕙草	In a desolate garden the basil withers,
音書絕	no message arrives.
嬌香絳質	The tender fragrance, the crimson body,
此際愁新遮	at this moment newly blocked by sorrow:
水深波浪闊	How deep the water and how wide the waves.
分付啼鶯	Instruct the calling nightingale
好迎錦繡芳節	better to welcome the sweet season of painted silks!

               *   *   *

胭脂添淚	Rouge skin drenched with tears
一向先成血	already turned to blood,[40]
瑤花融玉茗	Carnelian flowers dissolve jade tealeaves
神能接	for the spirits to receive.
紗櫥乍醒	On the satin chest I'm woken suddenly
腋下清風切	by the sharp touch of a breeze.
幽意憑誰說	With whom to share this feeling born of reclusion?
恨墨封題	I regret the ink has sealed this topic,
茜裙違夢淒別	indigo skirts forfeiting dream in anguished parting.

---

    39. 滿路花：詠紅茶. *Wenji* 623.
    40. It was said that King Du Yu of Shu grieved so deeply at losing his life and kingdom that his soul was transformed into the cuckoo, which would weep tears until it wept blood.

To the Tune of "Six Scoundrels": On Sleep[41]

Keats wrote in "Sleep and Poetry": "The very sense of where I was might well / Keep Sleep aloof: but more than that there came / Thought after thought to nourish up the flame / Within my breast." The masterpieces of poets are all written in fits of insomnia, and human civilization is only half of what it could be, since so much time is consumed by alluring sleep. Moreover, hearts cannot easily make impressions upon one another because sleep divides them. Only poets can communicate the meaning across this abyss.

漸宵深夢穩	Gradually night falls and I'm deep in peaceful dreams;
恨過隙	how I regret that swift as passing over a crevice
年光拋擲	the light of a year has been cast off.
夢難再留	A dream is hard to stay,
春風迴燕翼	spring winds turn back swallows on the wing,
忘返無跡	But I forget how to return, without any tracks to follow.
依樣心頭佔	As always my heart is occupied,
闌珊情緒	downcast in spirit,
似絮飄蕪國	like willow floss floating over a desolate land.
蘭襟沁處餘香澤	Where my orchid collar is drenched, a fragrance lingers.
繫馬金狨	I'll tie my horse with a golden marmoset saddle,
停車綺陌	pause my carriage on damask streets.[42]
玲瓏更誰堪惜	Who would not cherish such delicacy?
但鵑啼意亂	As soon as the cuckoo crows my thoughts are confused—
方寸仍隔	an inch away we are still so far apart.

* * *

閒庭人寂	I find myself in a serene courtyard with no sign of men,
接天芳草碧	the emerald of the flowers blending into the sky.
燈火綢謬際	The lantern fires are lined up one after another,
如瞬息	like a moment's breath.
都門冷落詞客	One writer of songs, all alone at the capital gate,
漫芳菲獨賞	appreciating alone those fragrant scents,
覓歡何極	searching for pleasure how can I reach it?

---

41. 六醜：睡. *Wenji* 615–616; *Ershi shiji shi da jia ci xuan* 287–288.
42. That is, streets as colorful and lively as damask.

思重整	I wish I could straighten
霧巾煙幘	my sash of fog and scarf of mist.
凝望裡	With concentrated gaze
自製離愁宛轉	I fashion intricate sorrows of separation
酒邊花側	out of wine and flowers.
琴心悄	A qin-like heart subtly
賦與流汐	writes for the flowing tides.
只睡鄉	But she is in the land of dreams,
兩地懸心遠	our hearts are far removed:
如何換得	what can I exchange for a moment there?

To the Tune of "Flower-Strewn Path": On the Self[43]

The Upanishads comment on the nature of the self that: "The mind is constantly lost amid the radiance of the self" and "The wise one seeks within himself." Yeats thought that all kinds of poetry reveal the self. But Xie Lingyun also wrote in his "Rhapsody on Dwelling in the Mountains," "How fortunate to have these days of idleness, in which to seek within myself." I agree with this, and how is writing lyrics any different?

聲隨雀噪乾	My voice amid the chittering of sparrows goes dry,
句壓櫻唇破	my verses bruise the cherry lips they press upon.[44]
香篝凉似水	The incense basket was cold as a stream
初添火	until I set it alight.
秋雲羅帕	Autumn clouds on the gauze handkerchief
鎮把愁紅裹	covering a flower-like face full of sorrow,
更萬千珍重	We say over and over again to take care,
一樹桃花	but the peach blossoms in the tree
笑人還要高臥	mock those who want to stay on a higher plane.[45]

* * *

迷離綺語	Bewildered by the damask phrases of romance,
作計何曾左	how have all my plans gone awry?
衰楊鴉蹴雪	Here among the withered poplars and snowbound crows,
侯門鎖	shut out from the gates of lords,
相思路上	Longing for you on my journey,
怕誤鈿車過	I fear I mistook the jeweled carriage that passed by.
盡詩中有我	In all of my poems there is an "I" somewhere,
自作纏綿	But I fashioned that sentiment myself,
但預防祖師呵	still hoping to prevent a rebuke from my Master.[46]

---

43. 滿路花：自我. *Wenji* 638; *Ershi shiji shi da jia ci xuan* 299–300.

44. I.e., the lips of the singing girl. Jao writes about the self indirectly by means of its entanglements in love affairs with others, which is after all the normal subject matter of the genre.

45. Literally "recline aloft," meaning to stay in reclusion away from worldly affairs, and romances.

46. According to a popular story, the Northern Song poet Huang Tingjian 黃庭堅 (1045–1105) was rebuked by Chan master Yuantong Xiu 圓通秀 (Huai Xian 懷賢 [1015–1082]) for writing "damask phrases" and not worrying about the condition of his soul and its destination after death. See *Xu chuan deng lu* 續傳燈錄 (*T* 2077: 51.615b).

To the Tune of "Jade Candles Renewed": On Spirit[47]

Lord Tao's poem about relieving the spirit dispatches feelings of joy or grief for a time, but it touches only the immediate moment, like expelling worry with a cup of ale, which can only be a temporary expedient.[48] Yet matter and energy are everlasting, filling up Heaven and Earth. As rotten grasses turn into fireflies, things are transformed only for a time. Thus when the spirit departs the body, it must find some resting place again. It is not the same as when the flame of the candle dies down: when the candle is exhausted, the light is gone too, but the flame leaves this candle and goes to burn on another one.[49] That the spirit is driven by the body, to be chopped and minced into nothing along with material things, vanishing so suddenly that men cannot even perceive it—what greater sorrow than this! I wrote a lyric to make sense of it.

中宵人醒後	When I wake at midnight
似幾點梅花	a few plum blossoms appear,
嫩苞新就	the tender petals barely opened.[50]
一時悟徹	In that moment I become aware
靈明處	of a spiritual radiance
渾把春心催漏	completely quelling the springlike heart in me.
紅蔫尚佇	The red petals still stand
有浩蕩光風相候	awaiting cool winds after the rain,
紺縷在	Damson strands abiding,
香送閒風	their fragrance is lifted in an idle breeze,
餘芬滿擷羅袖	the scent that lingers filling a gauze sleeve.

* * *

從知大塊無私	Thus I know that the Great Clod is impartial[51]
盡幻化同歸	for illusionary changes return to the same place.
惟神知否	Oh Spirit, do you understand?
好花似舊	Fine flowers are just as of old:

---

47. 玉燭新：神. *Wenji* 617; *Ershi shiji shi da jia ci xuan* 295–296.
48. The third part of "Body, Shadow, Spirit" 形影神, counseling indifference to worldly affairs, by the famous recluse poet Tao Qian 陶潛. Cf. Hightower, *The Poetry of T'ao Ch'ien*, 42–47.
49. Jao is adapting Du Bi's 杜弼 (?–559) argument that the spirit is much greater and longer-lasting than the body. See *Bei Qi shu* 24.352.
50. These images recall the story of the enchanting Princess Shouyang 壽陽, daughter of Song emperor Liu Yu 劉裕 (363–422), who fell asleep under a plum tree and woke up with plum blossoms in her hair that enhanced her beauty.
51. The "Great Clod" refers to Nature or the Fashioner of Things.

應只惜	They ought to pity us,
玉蕊未諳人瘦	the jade pistils that ignore our bodies' attenuation.
瓊枝乍秀	While carnelian branches have only just bloomed,
又轉眼	In hardly a glance,
飛蓬盈首	my hair has gone white as windswept tumbleweed.
信理亂難道無憑	Is there truly anything to rely on in the chaos of existence?
春簫又奏	Yet every spring the flutes play out once more.

Illustration 12. *Bamboo and Rock* (1995).

Bibliography

Selected Publications by Jao Tsung-i

Airs de Touen-houang / Touen-houang k'iu: Textes à chanter des VIIIe–Xe siècles manuscrits reproduits en fac-similé. With Paul Demiéville. Paris: Éditions du Centre national de la recherche scientifique, 1971.
Gu'an ci 固庵詞. Hong Kong: Privately published, 1968.
Gu'an shici xuan 固庵詩詞選. Beijing: Beijing tushuguan chubanshe, 2006.
Gu'an wenlu 固庵文錄. Taipei: Xin wenfeng chubanshe, 1989.
Jindong kaipi shishi 近東開闢史詩. Taipei: Xin wenfeng chubanshe, 1991.
Poèmes du lac noir [黑湖集]. Translated by Paul Demiéville. Originally published in *Asiatische Studien* 22 (1968). Rpt. Paris: École française d'extrême-orient, 2006.
Qing hui ji: Rao Zongyi yunwen, pianwen chuangzuo heji 清暉集：饒宗頤韻文、駢文創作合集. Shenzhen: Haitian chubanshe, 1999.
Rao Zongyi ershi shiji xueshu wenji 饒宗頤二十世紀學術文集. 20 volumes (14 *juan*). Taipei: Xin wenfeng, 2003.
Rao Zongyi yishu chuangzuo huiji 饒宗頤藝術創作匯集. Hong Kong: Jao Tsung-I Petite Ecole, University of Hong Kong, 2006.
Wenji: abbreviation for volume 20 (*juan* 14) of *Rao Zongyi ershi shiji xueshu wenji*, containing Jao's poetic oeuvre.
Wenxue yu shenming: Rao Zongyi fangtan lu 文學與神明：饒宗頤訪談錄. Interviews with Shi Yidui 施議對. Hong Kong: Sanlian shudian, 2010.
Xianggang daxue Rao Zongyi xueshuguan cangpin tulu I: Rao Zongyi jiaoshou yishu zuopin 香港大學饒宗頤學術館藏品圖錄I：饒宗頤教授藝術作品. Hong Kong: Jao Tsung-I Petite Ecole, University of Hong Kong, 2010.
Xuantang shiji pingzhu: Changzhou ji 選堂詩集評注：長洲集. Commentary by Chen Hanxi 陳韓曦 et al. Guangzhou: Huacheng chubanshe, 2011.
Yaoshan shicao 徭山詩草. 1945. Referred to in later sources as *Yaoshan ji* 瑤山集.

Selected Studies of Jao's Life and Poetry

Hu Xiaoming 胡曉明. *Rao Zongyi xueji* 饒宗頤學記. Hong Kong: Jao Tsung-I Petite Ecole, 1995.
Lam Lap 林立. "Xuantang xingshang ci zhi wo jian" 選堂形上詞之我見. *Huaxue* 9–10 (2008): 1811–1823.
Liu Mengfu 劉夢芙. "Lun *Xuantang yuefu*" 論選堂樂府. *Huaxue* 7 (2004): 62–77.
Shi Yidui 施議對. "Wei ershiyi shiji kaituo xin cijing, chuangzao xin citi—Rao Zongyi xingshang ci

fangtanlu" 為二十一世紀開拓新詞境，創造新詞體——饒宗頤形上詞訪談錄. *Wenxue yichan* 5 (1999): 106–114.

Yan Haijian 嚴海建. *Rao Zongyi zhuan: Xiangjiang hongru* 饒宗頤傳：香江鴻儒. Nanjing: Jiangsu renmin, 2012.

Zhao Songyuan 趙松元. "Yi shang gao qiu bai bu tong: lun Xuantang xiansheng de zheli shi" 一上高丘百不同：論選堂先生的哲理詩. *Hanshan shifan xueyuan xuebao* 3 (2001): 51–59.

Zhao Songyuan 趙松元, Liu Mengfu 劉夢芙, and Chen Wei 陳偉. *Xuantang shici lungao* 選堂詩詞論稿. Hefei: Huangshan shushe, 2009.

Zheng Weiming 鄭煒明. *Lun Rao Zongyi* 論饒宗頤. Hong Kong: Sanlian shudian, 1995.

Other Works Cited in Notes

Analects = *Lunyu* 論語. Cited by chapter and entry number.

Bai Juyi ji 白居易集. Beijing: Zhonghua shuju, 1979.

Baopuzi nei pian jiaoshi 抱朴子內篇校釋. Edited by Wang Ming 王明. Beijing: Zhonghua shuju, 1980.

Bei Qi shu 北齊書. Beijing: Zhonghua shuju, 1972.

Bei Qiong 貝瓊. *Qingjiang Bei xiansheng ji* 清江貝先生集. *Sibu congkan*.

Cai Zong-qi, ed. *How to Read Chinese Poetry: A Guided Anthology*. New York: Columbia University Press, 2008.

Chan, Timothy Wai Keung. "A Tale of Two Worlds: The Late Tang Poetic Presentation of the Romance of the Peach Blossom Font." *T'oung Pao* 94 (2008): 209–245.

Chaves, Jonathan. *The Columbia Book of Later Chinese Poetry*. New York: Columbia University Press, 1986.

Chen Zilong shiji 陳子龍詩集. Shanghai: Shanghai guji chubanshe, 1983.

Chuci buzhu 楚辭補注. Beijing: Zhonghua shuju, 1983.

Chunqiu Zuozhuan zhengyi 春秋左傳正義. See *Shisanjing zhushu*.

Davis, A.R. "The Double Ninth Festival in Chinese Poetry: A Study of Variations Upon a Theme." In Chow Tse-tsung, ed., *Wen-lin: Studies in the Chinese Humanities*, 44–64. Madison: University of Wisconsin Press, 1968.

Du Fu 杜甫. *Du shi xiangzhu* 杜詩詳注. Edited by Qiu Zhao'ao 仇兆鰲. Beijing: Zhonghua shuju, 1979.

Egan, Ronald. *Word, Image, and Deed in the Life of Su Shi*. Cambridge: Council on East Asian Studies, Harvard University, 1994.

Ershi shiji shi da jia ci xuan 二十世紀十大家詞選. Edited by Huang Zhaohan 黃兆漢 and Lam Lap 林立. Taipei: Xuesheng shuju, 2009.

Fang Hao 方豪. "Fang Yizhi he Tao shi shoujuan ji quanwen: guan Wang Xueting xiansheng jiu cang Fang Yizhi shou shu changjuan bayan" 方以智和陶詩手卷及全文：觀王雪艇先生舊藏方以智手書長卷跋言. *Dongfang zazhi* 7.7 (1974): 19–26.

Fang Yizhi 方以智. *Dong xi jun zhushi* 東西均注釋. Edited by Pang Pu 龐樸. Beijing: Zhonghua shuju, 2001.

Frazer, James. *The Golden Bough: The Third Edition*. 12 vols. London: Macmillan, 1932–1936.

Frodsham, J.D. *The Murmuring Stream: The Life and Works of the Chinese Nature Poet Hsieh Lingyün (385–433), Duke of K'ang-Lo.* 2 vols. Kuala Lumpur: University of Malaya Press, 1967.
Frodsham, J.D. *Goddesses, Ghosts, and Demons: The Collected Poems of Li He (790–816).* London: Anvil Press Poetry, 1983.
Fuller, Michael A. *The Road to East Slope: The Development of Su Shi's Poetic Voice.* Stanford: Stanford University Press, 1990.
Graham, A.C. *Poems of the Late T'ang.* Harmondsworth: Penguin Books, 1965. Rpt. New York: New York Review Books, 2008.
Graham, William T. *"The Lament for the South: Yü Hsin's 'Ai chiang-nan fu.'"* Cambridge: Cambridge University Press, 1990.
Guoyu 國語. Shanghai: Shanghai guji chubanshe, 1978.
Guang ya shuzheng 廣雅疏證. Shanghai: Shanghai guji chubanshe, 1983.
Hallam, Arthur Henry. *Remains in Verse and Prose: With a Preface and a Memoir.* London: John Murray, 1863.
Hightower, James R. *The Poetry of T'ao Ch'ien.* Oxford: Clarendon Press, 1970.
Holzman, Donald. *Poetry and Politics: The Life and Works of Juan Chi, A.D. 210–263.* Cambridge: Cambridge University Press, 1976.
Hou Han shu 後漢書. Beijing: Zhonghua shuju, 1965.
Huang Tingjian 黃庭堅. *Shangu neiji shizhu* 山谷內集詩注. *Congshu jicheng chubian.*
Ji yi ji 集異記. *Siku quanshu.*
Jin shu 晉書. Beijing: Zhonghua shuju, 1974.
Knechtges, David R. *The Han Rhapsody: A Study of the Fu of Yang Hsiung, 53 B.C.–A.D. 18.* Cambridge: Cambridge University Press, 1976.
Knechtges, David R. *Wen xuan, or Selections of Refined Literature,* vol. 1: *Rhapsodies on Metropolises and Capitals.* Princeton: Princeton University Press, 1982.
Knechtges, David R. *Wen xuan, or Selections of Refined Literature,* vol. 2: *Rhapsodies on Sacrifices, Hunting, Travel, Sightseeing, Palaces and Halls, Rivers and Seas.* Princeton: Princeton University Press, 1987.
Knechtges, David R. *Wen xuan, or Selections of Refined Literature,* vol. 3: *Rhapsodies on Natural Phenomena, Birds and Animals, Aspirations and Feelings, Sorrowful Laments, Literature, Music, And Passions.* Princeton: Princeton University Press, 1996.
Levenson, Joseph R. *Confucian China and Its Modern Fate: A Trilogy.* Berkeley: University of California Press, 1968.
Li Bai 李白. *Li Taibai quanji* 李太白全集. Edited by Wang Qi 王琦. Beijing: Zhonghua shuju, 1977.
Li ji zhengyi 禮記正義. See *Shisanjing zhushu.*
Liezi jishi 列子集釋. Edited by Yang Bojun 楊伯峻. Beijing: Zhonghua shuju, 1979.
Lin, Shuen-fu. *The Transformation of the Chinese Lyrical Tradition: Chiang K'uei and Southern Sung Tz'u Poetry.* Princeton: Princeton University Press, 1978.
Liu, James J.Y. *The Poetry of Li Shang-yin: Ninth-Century Baroque Chinese Poet.* Chicago: University of Chicago Press, 1969.
Liu, James J.Y. *Major Lyricists of the Northern Sung, A.D. 960–1126.* Princeton: Princeton University Press, 1974.
Lunheng jiaoshi 論衡校釋. Edited by Huang Hui 黃暉. Beijing: Zhonghua shuju, 1990.

Mao shi zhengyi 毛詩正義. See *Shisanjing zhushu*.
Mather, Richard B. *Shih-shuo hsin-yü: A New Account of Tales of the World*, 2nd ed. Ann Arbor: University of Michigan, Center for Chinese Studies, 2002.
Mei Tsu-lin and Kao Yu-kung. "Tu Fu's 'Autumn Meditations': An Exercise in Linguistic Criticism." *Harvard Journal of Asiatic Studies* 28 (1968): 44–80.
Mengzi zhushu 孟子注疏. See *Shisanjing zhushu*.
Mu Tianzi zhuan 穆天子傳. *Sibu congkan*.
Needham, Joseph. *Science and Civilisation in China*, Vol. V, Pt. 4: *Spagyrical Discovery and Invention: Apparatus and Theory*. With the collaboration of Lu Gwei-djen, and a contribution by Nathan Sivin. Cambridge: Cambridge University Press, 1980.
Nietzsche, Friedrich. *Also sprach Zarathustra*. In *Sämtliche Werke*, Band 4. Edited by Giorgio Colli und Mazzino Montinari. Berlin: Walter de Gruyter, 1999.
Nietzsche, Friedrich. *Nachgelassene Fragmente 1884–1885*. In *Sämtliche Werke*, Band 11. Edited by Giorgio Colli und Mazzino Montinari. Berlin: Walter de Gruyter, 1999.
Odes = *Shijing* 詩經, cited by poem and stanza number. See also Waley, *Book of Songs*.
Owen, Stephen. *The Great Age of Chinese Poetry: The High T'ang*. New Haven: Yale University Press, 1981.
Owen, Stephen. *An Anthology of Chinese Literature: Beginnings to 1911*. New York: Norton, 1996.
Owen, Stephen. *The Late Tang. Chinese Poetry of the Mid-Ninth Century (827–860)*. Cambridge: Harvard University Asia Center, 2006.
Pushkin, Aleksandr. *Eugene Onegin: A Novel in Verse*. Translated from the Russian, with a commentary by Vladimir Nabokov. Paperback edition in two volumes. Bollingen Series LXXII. Princeton: Princeton University Press, 1981.
Quan Tang shi 全唐詩. Beijing: Zhonghua, 1960.
Ren Daobin 任道斌. "Fang Yizhi de 'He Tao shi'" 方以智的和陶詩. *Wenxian* 1983.4: 14–20.
San guo zhi 三國志. Beijing: Zhonghua shuju, 1959.
Schmidt, J.D. *Within the Human Realm: The Poetry of Huang Zunxian, 1848–1905*. Cambridge: Cambridge University Press, 1994.
Schmidt, J.D. *The Poet Zheng Zhen (1806–1864) and the Rise of Chinese Modernity*. Leiden: Brill, 2013.
Shan hai jing jiaozhu 山海經校注. Edited by Yuan Ke 袁珂. Shanghai: Shanghai guji chubanshe, 1980.
Shangshu zhengyi 尚書正義. See *Shisanjing zhushu*.
Shi ji 史記. Beijing: Zhonghua shuju, 1959.
Shisanjing zhushu 十三經注疏. Originally published in 1815. Rpt. Taipei: Yiwen yinshuguan, 1980.
Shishuo xinyu 世說新語. Cited by chapter and anecdote number. Cf. Mather, *A New Account of Tales of the World*.
Shuo yuan jiaozheng 說苑校證. Beijing: Zhonghua shuju, 1987.
Strassberg, Richard E. *A Chinese Bestiary: Strange Creatures from the Guideways through Mountains and Seas*. Berkeley: University of California Press, 2002.
Su Shi 蘇軾. *Dongpo yuefu* 東坡樂府. Shanghai: Shanghai guji chubanshe, 1979.
Su Shi. *Su Shi shiji* 蘇軾詩集. Edited by Wang Wengao 王文誥 and Feng Yingliu 馮應榴. Taipei: Xuehai, 1983.

Su Shi. *Su Shi wenji* 蘇軾文集. Beijing: Zhonghua shuju, 1986.
T = *Taishō shinshō daizōkyō* 大正新修大藏經. Edited by Takakusu Junjirō 高楠順次郎, Watanabe Kaigyoku 渡邊海旭, et al. 100 vols. Tokyo: Taishō issaikyō kankōkai, 1924–1932.
Taiping guangji 太平廣記. Beijing: Zhonghua shuju, 1961.
Taiping yulan 太平御覽. Beijing: Zhonghua shuju, 1960.
Tian Xiaofei. "Muffled Dialect Spoken by Green Fruit: An Alternative History of Modern Chinese Poetry." *Modern Chinese Literature and Culture* 21.1 (2009): 1–45.
von Kowallis, Jon Eugene. *The Lyrical Lu Xun: A Study of His Classical-Style Verse*. Honolulu: University of Hawai'i Press, 1996.
von Kowallis, Jon Eugene. *The Subtle Revolution: Poets of the "Old Schools" during Late Qing and Early Republican China*. Berkeley: Institute of East Asian Studies, University of California Press, 2006.
Waley, Arthur. *The Book of Songs*. Edited with additional translations by Joseph R. Allen. 1937; rpt. New York: Grove Press, 1996.
Wang Jingwen gong shi jianzhu 王經文公詩箋註. Shanghai: Zhonghua shuju, 1958.
Wang Zi'an jizhu 王子安集注. Edited by Jiang Qingyi 蔣清翊. Shanghai: Shanghai guji, 1995.
Watson, Burton. *Japanese Literature in Chinese*. 2 vols. New York: Columbia University Press, 1975–1976.
Watson, Burton. *Zhuangzi: Basic Writings*. New York: Columbia University Press, 2003.
Wilhelm-Baynes = *The I Ching or Book of Changes*, Third Edition. Translated by Richard Wilhelm; rendered into English by Cary F. Baynes. Princeton: Princeton University Press, 1967.
Wixted, John Timothy. *Poems on Poetry: Literary Criticism by Yuan Hao-wen (1190–1257)*. Wiesbaden: Steiner, 1982.
Wu Shengqing. *Modern Archaics: Continuity and Innovation in the Chinese Lyric Tradition, 1900–1937*. Cambridge: Harvard University Asia Center, 2013.
Xie Lingyun ji jiaozhu 謝靈運集校註. Edited by Gu Shaobo 顧紹柏. Taipei: Liren shuju, 2004.
Xin Tang shu 新唐書. Beijing: Zhonghua shuju, 1975.
Yan Kejun 嚴可均 (1762–1843). *Quan shanggu Sandai Qin Han Sanguo Liuchao wen* 全上古三代秦漢三國六朝文. Taipei: Shijie shuju, 1969.
Yim, Lawrence C.H. *The Poet-Historian Qian Qianyi*. London: Routledge, 2009.
Yip, Wai-lim. *Ezra Pound's Cathay*. Princeton: Princeton University Press, 1969.
Yiwen leiju 藝文類聚. Shanghai: Shanghai guji chubanshe, 1982.
Yu Zishan jizhu 庾子山集注. Beijing: Zhonghua shuju, 1980.
Zhang Yan 張炎. *Ci yuan* 詞源. *Xuxiu siku quanshu*.
Zhang Yanyuan 張彥遠. *Lidai minghua ji* 歷代名畫記. *Congshu jicheng chubian*.
Zhanguo ce jianzheng 戰國策箋證. Shanghai: Shanghai guji chubanshe, 2006.
Zhou Bangyan 周邦彥. *Qingzhen ji jiaozhu* 清真集校注. Edited by Sun Hong 孫虹. Beijing: Zhonghua shuju, 2002.
Zhou yi zhengyi 周易正義. See *Shisanjing zhushu*.
Zhu Yizun shici xuanzhu 朱彝尊詩詞選注. Shanghai: Shanghai guji chubanshe, 1988.
Zhuangzi = *Zhuangzi jishi* 莊子集釋. Shanghai: Shanghai guji chubanshe, 1995.
Ziporyn, Brook. "Temporal Paradoxes: Intersections of Time Present and Time Past in the Song ci." *Chinese Literature: Essays, Articles, Reviews* 17 (1995): 89–109.

CORNELL EAST ASIA SERIES

4 Fredrick Teiwes, *Provincial Leadership in China: The Cultural Revolution and Its Aftermath*
8 Cornelius C. Kubler, *Vocabulary and Notes to Ba Jin's Jia: An Aid for Reading the Novel*
16 Monica Bethe & Karen Brazell, *Nō as Performance: An Analysis of the Kuse Scene of Yamamba.* Available for purchase: DVD by Monica Bethe & Karen Brazell, "Yamanba: The Old Woman of the Mountains"
18 Royall Tyler, tr., *Granny Mountains: A Second Cycle of Nō Plays*
23 Knight Biggerstaff, *Nanking Letters, 1949*
28 Diane E. Perushek, ed., *The Griffis Collection of Japanese Books: An Annotated Bibliography*
37 J. Victor Koschmann, Ōiwa Keibō & Yamashita Shinji, eds., *International Perspectives on Yanagita Kunio and Japanese Folklore Studies*
38 James O'Brien, tr., *Murō Saisei: Three Works*
40 Kubo Sakae, *Land of Volcanic Ash: A Play in Two Parts,* revised edition, tr. David G. Goodman
44 Susan Orpett Long, *Family Change and the Life Course in Japan*
48 Helen Craig McCullough, *Bungo Manual: Selected Reference Materials for Students of Classical Japanese*
49 Susan Blakeley Klein, *Ankoku Butō: The Premodern and Postmodern Influences on the Dance of Utter Darkness*
50 Karen Brazell, ed., *Twelve Plays of the Noh and Kyōgen Theaters*
51 David G. Goodman, ed., *Five Plays by Kishida Kunio*
52 Shirō Hara, *Ode to Stone,* tr. James Morita
53 Peter J. Katzenstein & Yutaka Tsujinaka, *Defending the Japanese State: Structures, Norms and the Political Responses to Terrorism and Violent Social Protest in the 1970s and 1980s*
54 Su Xiaokang & Wang Luxiang, *Deathsong of the River: A Reader's Guide to the Chinese TV Series Heshang,* trs. Richard Bodman & Pin P. Wan
55 Jingyuan Zhang, *Psychoanalysis in China: Literary Transformations, 1919-1949*
56 Jane Kate Leonard & John R. Watt, eds., *To Achieve Security and Wealth: The Qing Imperial State and the Economy, 1644-1911*
57 Andrew F. Jones, *Like a Knife: Ideology and Genre in Contemporary Chinese Popular Music*
58 Peter J. Katzenstein & Nobuo Okawara, *Japan's National Security: Structures, Norms and Policy Responses in a Changing World*

59 Carsten Holz, *The Role of Central Banking in China's Economic Reforms*
60 Chifumi Shimazaki, *Warrior Ghost Plays from the Japanese Noh Theater: Parallel Translations with Running Commentary*
61 Emily Groszos Ooms, *Women and Millenarian Protest in Meiji Japan: Deguchi Nao and Ōmotokyō*
62 Carolyn Anne Morley, *Transformation, Miracles, and Mischief: The Mountain Priest Plays of Kyōgen*
63 David R. McCann & Hyunjae Yee Sallee, tr., *Selected Poems of Kim Namjo*, afterword by Kim Yunsik
64 Hua Qingzhao, *From Yalta to Panmunjom: Truman's Diplomacy and the Four Powers, 1945–1953*
65 Margaret Benton Fukasawa, *Kitahara Hakushū: His Life and Poetry*
66 Kam Louie, ed., *Strange Tales from Strange Lands: Stories by Zheng Wanlong*, with introduction
67 Wang Wen-hsing, *Backed Against the Sea*, tr. Edward Gunn
69 Brian Myers, *Han Sōrya and North Korean Literature: The Failure of Socialist Realism in the DPRK*
70 Thomas P. Lyons & Victor Nee, eds., *The Economic Transformation of South China: Reform and Development in the Post-Mao Era*
71 David G. Goodman, tr., *After Apocalypse: Four Japanese Plays of Hiroshima and Nagasaki*, with introduction
72 Thomas Lyons, *Poverty and Growth in a South China County: Anxi, Fujian, 1949–1992*
74 Martyn Atkins, *Informal Empire in Crisis: British Diplomacy and the Chinese Customs Succession, 1927-1929*
76 Chifumi Shimazaki, *Restless Spirits from Japanese Noh Plays of the Fourth Group: Parallel Translations with Running Commentary*
77 Brother Anthony of Taizé & Young-Moo Kim, trs., *Back to Heaven: Selected Poems of Ch'ŏn Sang Pyŏng*
78 Kevin O'Rourke, tr., *Singing Like a Cricket, Hooting Like an Owl: Selected Poems by Yi Kyu-bo*
79 Irit Averbuch, *The Gods Come Dancing: A Study of the Japanese Ritual Dance of Yamabushi Kagura*
80 Mark Peterson, *Korean Adoption and Inheritance: Case Studies in the Creation of a Classic Confucian Society*
81 Yenna Wu, tr., *The Lioness Roars: Shrew Stories from Late Imperial China*
82 Thomas Lyons, *The Economic Geography of Fujian: A Sourcebook*, Vol. 1
83 Pak Wan-so, *The Naked Tree*, tr. Yu Young-nan
85 Cho Chong-Rae, *Playing With Fire*, tr. Chun Kyung-Ja
86 Hayashi Fumiko, *I Saw a Pale Horse and Selections from Diary of a Vagabond*, tr. Janice Brown

87 Motoori Norinaga, *Kojiki-den, Book 1*, tr. Ann Wehmeyer
88 Chang Soo Ko, tr., *Sending the Ship Out to the Stars: Poems of Park Je-chun*
89 Thomas Lyons, *The Economic Geography of Fujian: A Sourcebook*, Vol. 2
90 Brother Anthony of Taizé, tr., Midang: *Early Lyrics of So Chong-Ju*
92 Janice Matsumura, *More Than a Momentary Nightmare: The Yokohama Incident and Wartime Japan*
93 Kim Jong-Gil tr., *The Snow Falling on Chagall's Village: Selected Poems of Kim Ch'un-Su*
94 Wolhee Choe & Peter Fusco, trs., *Day-Shine: Poetry by Hyon-jong Chong*
95 Chifumi Shimazaki, *Troubled Souls from Japanese Noh Plays of the Fourth Group*
96 Hagiwara Sakutarō, *Principles of Poetry (Shi no Genri)*, tr. Chester Wang
97 Mae J. Smethurst, *Dramatic Representations of Filial Piety: Five Noh in Translation*
98 Ross King, ed., *Description and Explanation in Korean Linguistics*
99 William Wilson, *Hōgen Monogatari: Tale of the Disorder in Hōgen*
100 Yasushi Yamanouchi, J. Victor Koschmann and Ryūichi Narita, eds., *Total War and 'Modernization'*
101 Yi Chŏng-jun, *The Prophet and Other Stories*, tr. Julie Pickering
102 S.A. Thornton, *Charisma and Community Formation in Medieval Japan: The Case of the Yugyō-ha (1300-1700)*
103 Sherman Cochran, ed., *Inventing Nanjing Road: Commercial Culture in Shanghai, 1900–1945*
104 Harold M. Tanner, *Strike Hard! Anti-Crime Campaigns and Chinese Criminal Justice, 1979–1985*
105 Brother Anthony of Taizé & Young-Moo Kim, trs., *Farmers' Dance: Poems by Shin Kyŏng-nim*
106 Susan Orpett Long, ed., *Lives in Motion: Composing Circles of Self and Community in Japan*
107 Peter J. Katzenstein, Natasha Hamilton-Hart, Kozo Kato, & Ming Yue, *Asian Regionalism*
108 Kenneth Alan Grossberg, *Japan's Renaissance: The Politics of the Muromachi Bakufu*
109 John W. Hall & Toyoda Takeshi, eds., *Japan in the Muromachi Age*
110 Kim Su-Young, Shin Kyong-Nim, Lee Si-Young; *Variations: Three Korean Poets*; trs. Brother Anthony of Taizé & Young-Moo Kim
111 Samuel Leiter, *Frozen Moments: Writings on* Kabuki, *1966–2001*
112 Pilwun Shih Wang & Sarah Wang, *Early One Spring: A Learning Guide to Accompany the Film Video* February
113 Thomas Conlan, *In Little Need of Divine Intervention: Scrolls of the Mongol Invasions of Japan*
114 Jane Kate Leonard & Robert Antony, eds., *Dragons, Tigers, and Dogs: Qing Crisis Management and the Boundaries of State Power in Late Imperial China*

115 Shu-ning Sciban & Fred Edwards, eds., *Dragonflies: Fiction by Chinese Women in the Twentieth Century*
116 David G. Goodman, ed., *The Return of the Gods: Japanese Drama and Culture in the 1960s*
117 Yang Hi Choe-Wall, *Vision of a Phoenix: The Poems of Hŏ Nansŏrhŏn*
118 Mae J. Smethurst & Christina Laffin, eds., *The Noh* Ominameshi: *A Flower Viewed from Many Directions*
119 Joseph A. Murphy, *Metaphorical Circuit: Negotiations Between Literature and Science in Twentieth-Century Japan*
120 Richard F. Calichman, *Takeuchi Yoshimi: Displacing the West*
121 Fan Pen Li Chen, *Visions for the Masses: Chinese Shadow Plays from Shaanxi and Shanxi*
122 S. Yumiko Hulvey, *Sacred Rites in Moonlight: Ben no Naishi Nikki*
123 Tetsuo Najita & J. Victor Koschmann, *Conflict in Modern Japanese History: The Neglected Tradition*
124 Naoki Sakai, Brett de Bary, & Iyotani Toshio, eds., *Deconstructing Nationality*
125 Judith N. Rabinovitch & Timothy R. Bradstock, *Dance of the Butterflies: Chinese Poetry from the Japanese Court Tradition*
126 Yang Gui-ja, *Contradictions*, trs. Stephen Epstein and Kim Mi-Young
127 Ann Sung-hi Lee, *Yi Kwang-su and Modern Korean Literature*: Mujŏng
128 Pang Kie-chung & Michael D. Shin, eds., *Landlords, Peasants, & Intellectuals in Modern Korea*
129 Joan R. Piggott, ed., *Capital and Countryside in Japan, 300–1180: Japanese Historians Interpreted in English*
130 Kyoko Selden & Jolisa Gracewood, eds., *Annotated Japanese Literary Gems: Stories by Tawada Yōko, Nakagami Kenji, and Hayashi Kyōko* (Vol. 1)
131 Michael G. Murdock, *Disarming the Allies of Imperialism: The State, Agitation, and Manipulation during China's Nationalist Revolution, 1922–1929*
132 Noel J. Pinnington, *Traces in the Way: Michi and the Writings of Komparu Zenchiku*
133 Charlotte von Verschuer, *Across the Perilous Sea: Japanese Trade with China and Korea from the Seventh to the Sixteenth Centuries*, tr., Kristen Lee Hunter
134 John Timothy Wixted, *A Handbook to Classical Japanese*
135 Kyoko Selden & Jolisa Gracewoord, with Lili Selden, eds., *Annotated Japanese Literary Gems: Stories by Natsume Sōseki, Tomioka Taeko, and Inoue Yasushi* (Vol. 2)
136 Yi Tae-Jin, *The Dynamics of Confucianism and Modernization in Korean History*
137 Jennifer Rudolph, *Negotiated Power in Late Imperial China: The Zongli Yamen and the Politics of Reform*
138 Thomas D. Looser, *Visioning Eternity: Aesthetics, Politics, and History in the Early Modern Noh Theater*
139 Gustav Heldt, *The Pursuit of Harmony: Poetry and Power in Late Heian Japan*
140 Joan R. Piggott & Yoshida Sanae, *Teishinkōki: The Year 939 in the Journal of Regent Fujiwara no Tadahira*

141 Robert Bagley, *Max Loehr and the Study of Chinese Bronzes: Style and Classification in the History of Art*
142 Edwin A. Cranston, *The Secret Island and the Enticing Flame: Worlds of Memory, Discovery, and Loss in Japanese Poetry*
143 Hugh de Ferranti, *The Last Biwa Singer: A Blind Musician in History, Imagination and Performance*
144 Roger des Forges, Minglu Gao, Liu Chiao-mei, Haun Saussy, with Thomas Burkman, eds., *Chinese Walls in Time and Space: A Multidisciplinary Perspective*
145 Hye-jin Juhn Sidney & George Sidney, trs., *I Heard Life Calling Me: Poems of Yi Sŏng-bok*
146 Sherman Cochran & Paul G. Pickowicz, eds., *China on the Margins*
147 Wang Lingzhen & Mary Ann O' Donnell, trs., *Years of Sadness: Autobiographical Writings of Wang Anyi*
148 John Holstein, tr., *A Moment's Grace: Stories from Korea in Transition*
149 Sunyoung Park in collaboration with Jefferson J.A. Gatrall, trs., *On the Eve of the Uprising and Other Stories from Colonial Korea*
150 Brother Anthony of Taizé & Lee Hyung-jin, trs., *Walking on a Washing Line: Poems of Kim Seung-Hee*
151 Matthew Fraleigh, trs., with introduction, *New Chronicles of Yanagibashi and Diary of a Journey to the West: Narushima Ryūhoku Reports from Home and Abroad*
152 Pei Huang, *Reorienting the Manchus: A Study of Sinicization, 1583–1795*
153 Karen Gernant & Chen Zeping, *White Poppies and Other Stories by Zhang Kang-kang*
154 Mattias Burell & Marina Svensson, eds., *Making Law Work: Chinese Laws in Context*
155 Tomoko Aoyama & Barbara Hartley, trs., *Indian Summer by Kanai Mieko*
156 Lynne Kutsukake, tr., *Single Sickness and Other Stories by Masuda Mizuko*
157 Takako U. Lento, tr. with introduction, *Tanikawa Shuntarō: The Art of Being Alone, Poems 1952–2009*
158 Shu-ning Sciban & Fred Edwards, eds., *Endless War: Fiction & Essays by Wang Wen-hsing*
159 Elizabeth Oyler & Michael Watson, eds., *Like Clouds and Mists: Studies and Translations of Nō Plays of the Genpei War*
160 Michiko N. Wilson & Michael K. Wilson, trs., *Of Birds Crying by Minako Ōba*
161 Chifumi Shimazaki & Stephen Comee *Supernatural Beings from Japanese Noh Plays of the Fifth Group: Parallel Translations with Running Commentary*
162 Petrus Liu, *Stateless Subjects: Chinese Martial Arts Literature and Postcolonial History*
163 Lim Beng Choo, *Another Stage: Kanze Nobumitsu and the Late Muromachi Noh Theater*
164 Scott Cook, *The Bamboo Texts of Guodian: A Study and Complete Translation, Volume 1*
165 Scott Cook, *The Bamboo Texts of Guodian: A Study and Complete Translation, Volume 2*

166 Stephen D. Miller, translations with Patrick Donnelly, *The Wind from Vulture Peak: The Buddhification of Japanese Waka in the Heian Period*
167 Theodore Hughes, Jae-yong Kim, Jin-kyung Lee & Sang-kyung Lee, eds., *Rat Fire: Korean Stories from the Japanese Empire*
168 Ken C. Kawashima, Fabian Schäfer, Robert Stolz, eds., *Tosaka Jun: A Critical Reader*
169 John R. Bentley, *Tamakatsuma—A Window into the Scholarship of Motoori Norinaga*
170 Dandan Zhu, *1956: Mao's China and the Hungarian Crisis*
171 Hirokazu Miyazaki, ed., *Crisis and Hope: Experts and Intellectuals in Post-Fukushima Japan*
172 Sherman Cochran, ed., *The Capitalist Dilemma in China's Communist Revolution*
173 Kim Eunju tr., *Portrait of a Suburbanite: Poems of Choi Seung-ja*
174 Christina Laffin, Joan Piggott & Yoshida Sanae, *The Birth of Monarch: Selections from Fujiwara no Munetada's Journal Chūyūki*
175 J. Marshall Unger, Sangaku *Proofs: A Japanese Mathematician at Work*
176 Naoki Fukumori, *In Spring the Dawn: Sei Shōnagon's Makura no sōshi (The Pillow Book) and the Poetics of Amusement*
177 John B. Weinstein, *Voices of Taiwanese Women: Three Contemporary Plays*
178 Shu-ning Sciban & Ihor Pidhainy, eds., *Reading Wang Wenxing: Critical Essays*
179 Hou Xiaojia, *Negotiating Socialism in Rural China: Mao, Peasants, and Local Cadres in Shanxi, 1949–1953*
180 Joseph Esherick & Matthew Combs, eds., *1943: China at the Crossroads*
181 Rebecca Jennison & Brett de Bary, eds., *Still Hear The Wound: Toward an Asia, Politics, and Art to Come*
182 Nicholas Morrow Williams, *The Residue of Dreams: Selected Poems of Jao Tsung-i*
183 Bishop D. McKendree, *Barbed Wire and Rice: Poems and Songs from Japanese Prisoner-of-War Camps*

CORNELL East Asia Series

eap.einaudi.cornell.edu/publications

www.ingramcontent.com/pod-product-compliance
Lightning Source LLC
Chambersburg PA
CBHW060951230426
43665CB00015B/2153